VISION, TRACTION, HEALTHY

VISION, TRACTION, HEALTHY

ONE LEADER'S JOURNEY TO
LIVING THE EOS LIFE

A Get a Grip Prequel
The Origin Story of Alan Roth

Mark O'Donnell

E♦S
IMPACT

Printed in the United States of America

Published by Igniting Souls
PO Box 43, Powell, OH 43065
IgnitingSouls.com

LCCN: 2026903201
Paperback ISBN: 978-1-63680-624-2
Hardcover ISBN: 978-1-63680-625-9
e-Book ISBN: 978-1-63680-626-6

Available in paperback, hardcover, e-book, and audiobook.

Any Internet addresses (websites, blogs, etc.) and telephone numbers printed in this book are offered as a resource. They are not intended in any way to be or imply an endorsement by Igniting Souls, nor does Igniting Souls vouch for the content of these sites and numbers for the life of this book.

Some names and identifying details may have been changed to protect the privacy of individuals.

EOS®, The Entrepreneurial Operating System®, Traction®, and EOS Implementer® are registered trademarks owned by EOS Worldwide, LLC. For a complete list of trademarks owned by EOS Worldwide throughout this book, please visit branding.eosworldwide. com/eos-trademarks/.

The content of this book reflects the author's personal experiences, opinions, and interpretations. The inclusion of any individual, living or deceased, or any organization or entity, is not intended to malign, defame, or harm the reputation of such persons or entities. All statements regarding individuals are solely the author's perspective and do not represent verified facts unless expressly cited to a verifiable source.

The publisher has not independently investigated or confirmed the accuracy of any such references and disclaims all responsibility for them. Nothing in this book should be construed as factual assertions about the character, conduct, or reputation of any individual or entity mentioned. Any resemblance to persons living or dead is purely coincidental unless explicitly stated.

The publisher expressly disclaims liability for any alleged loss, damage, or injury arising from any perceived defamatory content or reliance upon statements within this work. Responsibility for the views, depictions, and representations rests solely with the author.

The superscript symbol IP listed throughout this book is known as the unique certification mark created and owned by Instant IP®. Its use signifies that the corresponding expression (words, phrases, chart, graph, etc.) has been protected by Instant IP® via smart contract. Instant IP® is designed with the patented smart contract solution (US Patent: 11,928,748), which creates an immutable time-stamped first layer and fast layer identifying the moment in time an idea is filed on the blockchain. This solution can be used in defending intellectual property protection. Infringing upon the respective intellectual property, i.e., IP, is subject to and punishable in a court of law.

"The path to mastery has no destination."

We stand on the shoulders of giants.
Gino Wickman, Don Tinney, Mike Paton:
We owe you a debt of gratitude.

CONTENTS

FOREWORD

AS IT DID for the characters in this book, EOS (the Entrepreneurial Operating System) came into my life when I needed it most. Frankly, that's true of nearly everyone in the EOS community. Professional Implementers like Alan Roth and Patrick Chen, business owners and leaders like Vic and Eileen from Swan Services, and the fine people who founded, own, or run the more than 30,000 companies that are now running their businesses on EOS.

My journey started after a colleague and friend asked me to run the market research firm she'd founded. I'd been excited enough by the opportunity to relocate my wife (who was expecting at the time) to Minneapolis. After just three days on the job, however, it started becoming very clear that I'd made a terrible mistake.

Our business was growing, generating a healthy profit, and serving its clients well, but our founder was exhausted and frustrated. Poaching me from another company hadn't been easy or inexpensive, so she rightly expected me to immediately make a positive difference—in her business and her life.

I failed.

On paper, this was a perfect opportunity. We had been business partners for several years. We'd sold and delivered some impressive projects together. I brought the right capabilities, track record, and tireless work ethic to the role. I saw the potential in her company and believed that I could help unlock it. It seemed like a perfect fit.

It wasn't. Despite working around the clock, trying everything to make positive changes happen quickly, I was clearly failing to earn the founder's trust. I was terrified, exhausted, and had almost no time or energy for my wife and newborn son. For the first time in my career, I was stuck, frustrated, and terrified.

When an entrepreneur from across the street introduced me to a "way of operating" an entrepreneurial company that he'd learned from Gino Wickman, I was intrigued. The tools and disciplines he shared seemed simple, practical, and timeless. Some of the concepts and tactics were very similar to things I'd already suggested to our founder, only to be summarily rejected. A month later, after reading Traction, I was on the phone with Gino's business partner, Don Tinney. Three months after that, I found myself in Livonia, Michigan, at "Boot Camp" learning how to become a Professional EOS Implementer.

Don had recruited me after my neighbor introduced us. He and Gino were recruiting people like me because they wanted to share EOS with entrepreneurs around the world. Gino had painstakingly built and refined the Model, Toolbox, and Process over seven years of helping entrepreneurial leadership teams in SE Michigan. Don had proven that someone other than Gino could be successful in helping teams implement EOS to get more of what they want from their businesses.

"We're looking for people like you to help us put a huge dent in the universe," Don had said on the phone, "one entrepreneurial company at a time."

"Is this a cult?" I thought. "Is this another 'opportunity' that's just a road to ruin?"

The company had no website or online presence of any kind. Nobody I knew had ever heard of EOS (except my neighbor, who rarely wore shoes). I sought counsel from my father-in-law, thinking he'd grab me by both ears and pound some sense into me. Instead, he helped me understand that the only real risk in life is betting on someone other than oneself.

"Open your own lemonade stand," he said. "Work your ass off. Study with the masters. Spend your days and nights learning to make better lemonade than anyone else. Tell the world about it. Rely on yourself!"

So, I did. But I was still terrified.

Boot Camp was free, mind you. We had to cover travel costs—for me, a flight, a rental car, and two nights at a run-down Holiday Inn across the parking lot from Gino's office. His session room was spare—no visible technology, just a conference room setup with big whiteboards on the front and back walls. This was clearly a bootstrapped operation run by two humble, passionate, hard-working entrepreneurs.

After the four of us "boot campers" introduced ourselves, the learning commenced. Gino presented EOS Worldwide's V/TO (Vision/Traction Organizer) one section at a time. Our Core Values, our Core Focus, and then our 10-Year Target.

"10,000 companies running on EOS by 2020," he declared.

A fellow student asked what "running on EOS" meant. Ready for the question, Gino explained that it meant the company's leadership team had hired one of us to help them embark on the EOS Implementation journey. I looked around the room, did a little math, and raised my hand.

"How many clients are running on EOS today?" I asked.

Gino and Don looked at each other, each of them clearly doing a little of their own math. They conferred for a moment, and Gino said with confidence:

"61."

"61?!" I replied, trying hard (and probably failing) to avoid sounding incredulous. "How the heck are you gonna get to 10,000?"

Gino thought for a moment. There appeared to be no offense taken, no desire to put me in my place.

"We have no idea," he said calmly. "It's what I want, and it's what Don wants, and we both believe it's possible. We also believe that, when you write a big goal down, focus on it every day, and tell as many people about it as you can, you'll attract other talented, hard-working people who want and believe in the same thing. And that—together—we'll figure it out one quarter at a time."

That calm, humble answer (and a little divine intervention) made me certain I'd made the right choice. This was a vision I could believe in, and a community I desperately wanted to be a part of. It was clear that this was everything Gino and Don thought it could be, and that if I worked hard, stayed humble, and committed to the lifelong journey to mastery that lay ahead, we could achieve great things together.

That turned out to be true, but it hasn't been easy, and it's not for everyone.

As with all journeys to achieve something special, succeeding as an EOS Implementer requires focus, discipline, accountability, and resilience.

More than anything else, that's what you need to take from *Vision, Traction, Healthy*. The life and work of an EOS Implementer is infinitely rewarding—financially and emotionally. But it's hard. It's humbling. To be successful, you may need to unlearn much of what you know and start from scratch.

You must believe in entrepreneurship and genuinely want to help business owners and leaders run better businesses and live better lives. You must devote yourself to a lifelong journey to mastery. That means learning to teach, coach, and facilitate the way a master EOS Implementer does it. It means studying the tools, concepts, and techniques forever, even if you're the person who wrote the Implementer Guide or recorded the training video.

It means loving and helping your fellow EOS Implementers rather than competing against them. It means giving freely of your time when a client, a colleague, or a friend needs help. It means doing the right thing, even when it's hard.

Most of all, it requires you to work hard every day at being the very best EOS Implementer you can be. This is hard for a lot of entrepreneurs—we can be easily distracted and get bored with repetition. But it's always been enough for me. And if you devote yourself fully to this work and "stay focused," I can promise it'll always be enough for you, too.

Before you enjoy the book, let me finish that story about my first Boot Camp, and our journey to 10,000 and beyond. Fast forward eight years. Gino and I are about 2 ½ years into a 3-year succession plan, and I'm attending EOS Worldwide's Annual Planning Session as its new Visionary (with Don as our Integrator). Gino is facilitating in the very same session room, though by then we'd upgraded to a slightly better hotel.

Again, we get to our 10-Year Target, and I ask, "Where are we now?"

Some papers shuffle, and I hear "2,132" or some number that felt nowhere NEAR close enough to 10,000.

"Whoa, so do we need to change it?!" After all, I now feel the tremendous weight of accountability for achieving our vision and hitting that number. My pulse was racing.

Don weighed in, sharing signs he and the rest of the team had seen that our flywheel was turning, and momentum was on our side. I reluctantly agreed with the decision to leave it unchanged.

Fully committed to that aggressive goal, our amazing leadership team dug in and worked hard to stimulate progress and preserve the core. We needed to accelerate growth without compromising what made EOS and our Implementer Community so special. By February 2017, my panic had subsided, and we all felt so confident that we agreed to change our

10-Year Target to a more aggressive goal: 100,000 companies running on EOS by 2030.

What's truly remarkable, though, is when EOSW hit that original 10-year Target—the one Gino first wrote down at the Starbucks during a Clarity Break before he'd even met Don and started recruiting Implementers.

EOS Worldwide hit 10,000 companies in **October of 2020!** How?

With a crystal clear and compelling vision, shared by a small band of brothers and sisters who see it, believe in it, and want to be a part of it. For 18 years, we've been working together to figure it out, one quarter (and one entrepreneurial leadership team) at a time.

If you'd like to help us make a huge dent in the universe and are willing to engage fully in this lifelong journey to mastery, I hope you'll join us.

—Mike Paton
Author of *Get a Grip*

PROLOGUE

The Card

"You never know which small gift will become
someone else's turning point."

THE WEIGHT HIT John Fredrickson the moment he stepped out of his truck. Not a physical weight, but the kind that settles behind your eyes after weeks of three-hour nights and seventy-hour work weeks. The kind that makes walking into a room full of successful people feel like wading through concrete.

He pushed through the lobby doors of the hotel, already regretting the decision to come. Another networking event. Another evening of pretending everything was fine.

That's when Eileen Sharp spotted him.

She was helping Bill Pullian check members into the Business Roundtable social event when she glanced up and saw John crossing the lobby. His shoulders were hunched forward, his jaw tight. The vein on his temple pulsed visibly even from twenty feet away. He moved like a man carrying something heavy that no one else could see.

Eileen knew that walk. She had walked it herself three years ago.

"Hey, John," she said, stepping away from the registration table and extending both arms for a hug. "Everything okay?"

John's face flushed red. He leaned in for a lukewarm embrace, barely making contact.

"Hey, Eileen," he mumbled. "To be honest, I've been better."

She had known John for years through these Roundtable events. He ran Fredrickson Construction, a commercial building company much larger than her own Swan Services. Successful by any external measure. But right now, standing in this hotel lobby in a rumpled sport coat, he looked like a man on the edge of something.

Eileen grabbed his hand and pulled him toward the bar. "Then let me buy you a drink, and you can tell me all about it."

A few minutes later, they sat in a quiet corner of the lobby, drinks in hand. John stared into his bourbon as if it held answers.

"What's going on?" Eileen asked. Not the polite networking version of the question. The real one.

John laughed bitterly. "It's the same old stuff. We're doing okay on paper, but I'm working way too hard, and it seems like I spend most of every day ticked off at someone or something."

"Like what?" Eileen leaned forward. "Or whom?"

"Oh, you know." John waved his hand dismissively. "I'm ticked off at my people. None of them really seems to get it or even to really care. We've stopped growing, and we're not making anywhere near enough money for a company our size. Frankly, I feel like I've lost control of the business, and no matter what I try, nothing seems to work. Blah, blah, blah."

He took a long pull of bourbon.

Eileen sat back, a knowing smile forming at the corners of her mouth. "Come on, John. I've been there. I really do want to help, even if you just need somebody to listen."

Something in her eyes told John she meant it. And something in him cracked open.

He poured out his guts.

Eleven years he'd been building this company. Started from nothing, just his own strong will and determination. The first eight years had been hard but fun. He was making something, proving something, growing something. But the last three years had been brutal.

Seventy-hour weeks had become normal. He lay awake most nights running through everything he hadn't had time to fix that day. His leadership team, if you could call them that, was a revolving door of internal promotions that didn't work out and external hires that didn't stick. He'd burned through consultants like kindling. Nothing changed. Nothing lasted.

"I wouldn't call any of them real leaders," John said, his voice hollow. "And we've never even gotten close to functioning as a team. I know it's my fault. Frankly, in this condition, I can't be an easy guy to work for."

He finished his bourbon, setting the glass down harder than he intended.

"Honestly, Eileen, if I can't figure this out, I'm going to sell the damn company and start over."

Eileen let the words settle. She watched John stare at the empty glass, saw the defeat in his shoulders, and recognized the exhaustion that went deeper than lack of sleep.

"Believe it or not," she said, smiling broadly, "I know exactly what that feels like."

John looked up.

"Three years ago, at an event just like this one, a good friend did something for me that I'll never forget."

Eileen reached into her purse. Her fingers found the business card easily. She'd carried it for years now, the edges worn soft, the corners rounded from handling. She pulled it out and held it for a moment, remembering.

Then she grabbed a pen from her bag and wrote something on the back of the card. She slid it across the table to John.

"On your way home tonight," she said, her voice firm with a certainty that surprised him, "I want you to call my friend Alan Roth. If you really want to start getting everything you want from your business, I promise he can help you."

John picked up the card. Plain white stock. Simple black text.

Alan Roth
EOS Implementer

Below that, a phone number. And at the bottom, a single word:

Traction

He flipped the card over to read what Eileen had written. Her handwriting was quick but clear:

Alan helped change everything. Trust me.

When John looked up, Eileen was already gone. He spotted her across the lobby, rushing to greet a tall man who must have been her husband. She wrapped her arms around him with the easy affection of a woman who had her life in order. A woman who slept through the night.

John examined the card again. Alan Roth. EOS Implementer. Traction.

He had no idea what any of it meant.

But Eileen Sharp was one of the sharpest entrepreneurs he knew. Her company had transformed over the past few years. He'd watched from afar as Swan Services went from a scrappy operation to something that seemed to run like a machine. Eileen herself had changed, too. Less frantic. More present. She'd stopped missing Roundtable events. Started actually enjoying them.

Whatever this Alan Roth had done for her, it was real.

John slipped the card into his jacket pocket. He'd call on the drive home. Or maybe tomorrow.

He ordered another bourbon and watched the room fill with entrepreneurs laughing, networking, and making deals. Most of them were probably lying about how well things were going. He'd done it himself for years.

But Eileen hadn't lied. She'd handed him a lifeline.

He changed everything.

John finished his drink and headed for the door.

* * *

What John Fredrickson didn't know, as he walked to his car and pulled out his phone to dial the number on that worn business card, was that Alan Roth had once been exactly where John was now.

Lost. Frustrated. Working himself to death for a company that seemed to be working against him.

This is the story of how Alan Roth found his way out.

And how he dedicated his life to helping others do the same.

1

The Ceiling

---

*"You can't power through a ceiling.
You can only bang your head against it until
something breaks."*

Ten years earlier...

THE RESIGNATION LETTER sat on Alan Roth's desk like an accusation.

He read it again, though he'd already memorized the key phrases. *Pursuing other opportunities. Time for a change. Grateful for everything I've learned.* The professional language of someone who couldn't wait to get out.

This was his third operations director in four years.

Alan pushed back from his desk and stared out the window at the parking lot of Roth Talent Solutions. Forty-five employees. Eight million in revenue. Fifteen years of his life poured into this company, and he couldn't keep an ops director for more than eighteen months.

He knew what his leadership team would say. They'd blame the candidates. Wrong fit. Not ready for the role. Couldn't handle the pressure. But Alan had hired these people himself. He'd vetted them carefully, checked references, and trusted his gut. Three times now, his gut had been wrong.

Or maybe the problem wasn't the candidates at all.

His phone buzzed. Text from his assistant: *Hensley on line 2. Says it's urgent.*

Hensley Technologies. Their largest client. Alan picked up the receiver, already bracing himself.

"Bill, what can I do for you?"

"Alan, we need to talk about the Riverside project."

Twenty minutes later, Alan hung up the phone with a knot in his stomach. Hensley wasn't happy. The project was behind schedule, the communication had been poor, and Bill was "evaluating options." That was client-speak for *we're thinking about firing you.*

Alan walked to his door and looked out at the open floor plan. His people were busy. Phones ringing, keyboards clicking, the hum of a company in motion. From the outside, it probably looked like success. Eight million dollars. Forty-five jobs. A building with their name on it.

From the inside, it felt like drowning.

* * *

The leadership team meeting started at 2 p.m., which meant it actually started at 2:15 because Greg, his sales director, was perpetually late, and nobody could start without sales numbers.

Alan sat at the head of the conference table, watching his team trickle in. Karen from finance arrived first, as always, her laptop already open to a spreadsheet she'd been stress-refreshing since 6 a.m. Marcus from recruiting shuffled in next, coffee in one hand, phone in the other, his attention somewhere else entirely. Diane from HR clutched a folder thick with problems, her eyes already searching for someone else to hand them to.

And finally Greg, breezing in fifteen minutes late with a fresh coffee and the easy grin of a man who believed charm could substitute for punctuality.

"Sorry, sorry," Greg said, not sounding sorry at all. "Got caught up with a prospect."

"Let's get started," Alan said. "We've got a lot to cover."

The conference room smelled like stale coffee and dry-erase markers, the particular scent of meetings that solved nothing.

What followed was ninety minutes of everything Alan had come to dread about these meetings. Karen reported that margins were down again, then immediately blamed sales for discounting too heavily. Greg fired back that they wouldn't need to discount if recruiting could actually fill positions on time. Marcus defended his team by pointing out that the job specs kept changing mid-search. Everyone talked. Nobody listened. Nothing got resolved.

Alan tried to steer the conversation toward solutions, but every attempt dissolved into finger-pointing. When he pushed for accountability, he got excuses. When he demanded commitments, he got vague promises that everyone knew wouldn't be kept.

By 3:30, they had discussed a dozen issues and solved none of them. Alan called the meeting to a close, and his team scattered like inmates granted parole.

He sat alone in the conference room, staring at the whiteboard covered in half-finished action items and orphaned bullet points.

This was his company. He had built it from nothing. And somehow, he had lost control of it completely.

* * *

The rest of the afternoon was a blur of small fires.

A recruiter quit without notice, leaving several client searches understaffed. A vendor called about an overdue invoice that Alan had never seen. Two employees got into an argument loud enough to be heard across the floor, and Diane from HR was nowhere to be found.

Alan handled each crisis the only way he knew how: by stepping in and doing it himself. He reassigned the project work. He tracked down the invoice and authorized payment. He separated the arguing employees and delivered a lecture about professionalism that he knew wouldn't stick.

By six o'clock, he was exhausted. By seven, he was still at his desk, answering emails that should have been handled by other people. By eight, he was the last one in the building, the parking lot empty except for his car.

He thought about calling Sarah. They'd had dinner plans, hadn't they? Or was that last week? The days blurred together. He couldn't remember the last time he'd made it home before she went to bed. Couldn't remember the last time they'd had a real conversation about something other than his work stress.

He sent her a text instead: *Running late. Don't wait up.*

The three dots appeared, then disappeared. No response came.

* * *

Alan pulled into his driveway at 9:15. The house was dark except for the bedroom window, where a faint blue glow suggested Sarah was watching television. Or maybe just lying awake, waiting for him to come home.

He sat in the car for a long moment, engine off, staring at the house he'd bought with the success of his company. Four bedrooms. A yard that a landscaping service maintained because he never had time. A life that looked perfect from the outside.

Inside, he moved quietly through the kitchen, grabbed a beer from the refrigerator, and settled into his home office to review tomorrow's calendar. More meetings. More fires. More of the same.

The ceiling, they called it. He'd read about it in business books, heard other entrepreneurs talk about it at conferences. That invisible barrier that growing companies hit, where everything that got you here stops working, and you can't figure out how to get to the next level.

Alan had always thought he'd power through it. That was what he did. He worked harder than anyone, solved problems that stumped his team, and willed his company forward through sheer determination.

But you can't power through a ceiling. He was learning that now. You can only bang your head against it until something breaks.

He finished his beer and climbed the stairs to the bedroom. Sarah was asleep, or pretending to be. He brushed his teeth, changed clothes, and slid into bed beside her.

Then he lay awake until two in the morning, running through everything he hadn't fixed, everything that would be waiting for him tomorrow, everything that was slowly falling apart despite his best efforts.

* * *

The Business Roundtable met on the third Thursday of every month.

Alan had been a member for six years, part of a group of eight business owners who met to share challenges, offer advice, and hold each other accountable. In theory, it was a safe space for honest conversation. In practice, Alan had become skilled at presenting the polished version of his struggles. Challenges that were manageable. Problems with clear solutions. The kind of issues that made him look thoughtful rather than desperate.

But today, something cracked.

They were going around the table, each member sharing updates, when Alan's turn came. He started with the usual framing: revenue was solid, working through some operational challenges, exploring new market opportunities.

Then Paul, who sat across the table, raised an eyebrow.

"Alan, that's the same update you've given for the last six months. What's really going on?"

The room went quiet. The unwritten rule of the forum was that you didn't push too hard. But Paul had known Alan for years, and he wasn't one for pretense.

Alan felt the facade crumble.

"Honestly? I'm drowning."

The words came out before he could stop them. And once he started, he couldn't stop.

He told them about the revolving door of operations directors. About the leadership team that couldn't get aligned on anything. About Hensley threatening to leave and the dozen other clients who'd become problems instead of partners. About the eighty-hour weeks and the sleepless nights and the marriage he was neglecting.

"We've been stuck at eight million for three years," Alan said. "Revenue's flat. Margins are shrinking. I've tried everything. New hires, consultants, restructuring, incentive programs. Nothing sticks. I feel like I'm running on a treadmill that keeps speeding up, and I can't figure out how to get off."

The room was silent when he finished. Alan stared at the table, embarrassed by his own honesty.

Finally, Paul spoke.

"How long have you felt like this?"

"Years," Alan admitted. "But it's gotten worse. A lot worse."

"Have you thought about getting help? Real help, not just another consultant?"

Alan laughed bitterly. "I've been through three consultants in the last four years. They come in, do their assessments, hand me a report full of recommendations, and cash their checks. Six months later, nothing's changed."

"This would be different," Paul said.

"That's what they all say."

"No, I mean it." Paul leaned forward. "My brother's company was in a similar spot a few years ago. Stuck, frustrated, with the leadership team in chaos. He brought in a woman who completely transformed the business. Not with some fancy framework or theoretical model. Just simple, practical tools that actually worked."

"A consultant," Alan said flatly.

"That's the thing. She's not a consultant. She calls herself an Implementer. She doesn't just tell you what to do and walk away. She teaches you a system and works with you until it sticks."

Alan shook his head. "Paul, I appreciate it, but I've heard this pitch before."

"I know you have. So had my brother. He almost didn't call her because of it." Paul pulled out his phone, scrolled for a moment, then looked back up at Alan. "But he did call. And eighteen months later, his company was unrecognizable. Revenue up forty percent. Margins doubled. And here's the thing: he actually enjoys running it now. He's home for dinner. He takes vacations. He's got his life back."

Alan wanted to dismiss it. He'd been burned too many times by promises like this. But something in Paul's voice was different. This wasn't a casual recommendation. This was Paul, who never oversold anything, telling him there was a way out.

"What's her name?" Alan asked.

"Sue Hawkes. She's local, right here in Minneapolis." Paul wrote something on a napkin and slid it across the table. "Call her. Tell her I sent you. Give her ninety minutes. If you don't see anything different, you've lost an hour and a half. But if my brother's experience is any indication, it'll be the most important ninety minutes of your business career."

Alan looked at the napkin. A name. A phone number. A life-line, maybe. Or maybe just another expensive disappointment.

"What does she do that's so different?" Alan asked.

Paul smiled. "She's got this system. Simple, practical tools for running a business. She teaches it to you and your team, and then she holds you accountable for implementing it. No reports. No theory. Just real stuff that works."

"That's it?"

"That's it. But here's the thing." Paul paused, choosing his words carefully. "It's not magic. It's hard work. You have to be willing to look at everything honestly. Your structure, your people, your own role. Some of it's going to be uncomfortable. But if you commit to it, really commit, it works."

Alan folded the napkin and put it in his pocket.

"I'll think about it," he said.

But even as he said the words, he knew he would call. Because the alternative was another year of this. Another year of eighty-hour weeks and sleepless nights, and a company that was slowly grinding him down.

He'd tried everything else.

What did he have to lose?

2

The Different One

"Help First is not just a slogan.
It's how we win."

ALAN ALMOST DIDN'T make the call.

He sat in his office the morning after the Business Roundtable meeting, Paul's napkin smoothed flat on his desk, and stared at the phone number. Sue Hawkes. The woman who wasn't a consultant.

Three times he picked up the receiver. Three times, he put it back down.

He'd been here before. The initial excitement of a new solution, followed by weeks of meetings and assessments, followed by a report full of recommendations that sat on his shelf gathering dust. He had a whole stack of those reports. Strategic plans. Organizational assessments. Leadership development frameworks. Expensive paperweights, all of them.

But Paul's words kept echoing: Eighteen months later, his company was unrecognizable.

Alan picked up the phone a fourth time and dialed.

"This is Sue Hawkes."

The voice was calm, unhurried. Not the polished pitch of a saleswoman.

"Sue, this is Alan Roth. Paul Harrison asked me to call you regarding your services."

"Alan, yes. Paul mentioned you might reach out. I'm looking forward to discussing your business with you. Do you mind if I briefly tell you what I do first?"

"Sure."

"I help people get what they want from their businesses. I do that by providing a complete system with simple tools to help you do three things we call vision, traction, and healthy."

Alan grabbed a pen, more out of habit than expectation.

"Vision," Sue continued, "from the standpoint of getting your leaders 100 percent on the same page with where your organization is going and how it's going to get there. Traction means helping your leaders become more disciplined and accountable, and executing well to achieve every part of your vision. And healthy, meaning helping your leaders become a healthy, functional, cohesive leadership team. Because, unfortunately, leaders often don't function well as a team."

Alan thought about the finger-pointing in his conference room. The meetings that solved nothing. The leadership team that couldn't agree on anything.

"From there," Sue said, "as goes your leadership team, so goes the rest of your organization. We get to the point where your entire organization is crystal clear on your vision, all much more disciplined and accountable, executing well, gaining consistent traction, and advancing as a healthy, functional, cohesive team."

The words landed differently than the usual consultant jargon. Simple. Direct. No buzzwords.

"If any of that resonates with you," Sue said, "the first step is a 90-Minute Meeting to show you what EOS is and how it works. Would you like to schedule it?"

Alan hesitated. Ninety minutes. His calendar was already packed. But something in Sue's voice, the lack of pressure, the straightforward explanation, made him want to know more.

"What would we cover in ninety minutes?"

"I'll walk you and your leadership team through the system and the tools. By the end, we'll both be able to determine if there's a fit. And the meeting is completely free. I'm giving you ninety minutes of my time to show you how this works."

Alan had sat through plenty of free sales pitches before. But this didn't feel like a pitch. It felt like an offer to help.

"When can we meet?"

They settled on a date two weeks out. Sue asked Alan to bring his entire leadership team, recommended they meet in her office to avoid distractions, and confirmed she'd have whiteboards available.

After they hung up, Alan stared at the phone for a long moment. Vision, traction, healthy. Three simple words. He'd built an eight-million-dollar company, and he wasn't sure he had any of them.

* * *

Two weeks later, Alan pulled into the parking lot of a modest office building in suburban Minneapolis. His leadership team followed in separate cars: Karen, Marcus, Diane, and Greg. He'd told them only that they were meeting with someone who might be able to help with their operational challenges. He hadn't used the word consultant.

Sue Hawkes stood at the door, greeting each person as they entered. She was tall, maybe five-foot-ten, with long dark hair and an athletic build. Her smile was warm and immediate, the kind that made you feel like you'd known her for years. She looked to be around fifty, and she shook hands firmly but without the aggressive grip that Alan associated with salespeople.

The session room surprised Alan. The walls were painted a bold orange, and the Entrepreneurial Operating System (EOS) logo was prominently displayed. A large table surrounded by comfortable chairs filled the center of the room. But what struck him most was what wasn't there. No big television screen. No projector. No laptops or tablets set up for a slick presentation. Just whiteboards mounted on three walls, waiting to be filled.

Greg noticed it too. "No PowerPoint?" he muttered to Alan as they took their seats.

"Apparently not," Alan said. He wasn't sure if that was a good sign or a bad one.

Once everyone was seated, Sue began.

"Welcome, and good morning. Thank you for giving me ninety minutes of your precious time. This meeting is known as the 90-Minute Meeting, which means we will be together for about... ninety minutes."

A few people chuckled. Karen looked skeptical. Greg checked his phone.

Sue noticed Greg's distraction and addressed it with a warm but firm smile. "Before we dive in," she said, catching his eye, "I have one request. To make the most of our time together, I ask that we keep this a 'device-free' zone. If we can all give each other our undivided attention for these ninety minutes, we'll accomplish much more. Is everyone okay with that?"

Greg nodded and tucked his phone into his pocket.

"Thank you," Sue continued.

"During the ninety minutes, there are four very specific points we cover. We find that this is the best and fastest way for us to transfer information, get on the same page, and ultimately determine whether or not there is a fit here."

She held up one finger. "Step one is About Us. I'll share a little information about EOS and about me, so you know I'm not here practicing on you." A second finger. "Step two is About You. I'm going to turn the tables on you. I want to learn

where you've been, where you are, and where you're going."
A third finger. "Step three, we call The Tools. This is where
I'm going to open my toolbox and share with you the specific
tools we use to help our clients get more of what they want
from their businesses." A fourth finger. "And step four is The
Process. I'm going to share with you exactly how I work with
my clients and their leadership teams to implement EOS in
their businesses."

Sue paused and looked around the room.

"Those are the four steps. Any questions before we begin?"

"Are we going right to 11:30?" Karen asked. "I have a call
at that time."

"I'll make sure we conclude right at 11:30, Karen," Sue
replied immediately.

* * *

"Everything I'm going to share with you today was created by
a lifelong entrepreneur by the name of Gino Wickman," Sue
began. "He's been an entrepreneur since the age of twenty-one.
At twenty-five, he was called in to run his family business
and found that it was in need of a turnaround. He worked with
the leadership team to turn the company around over about
three years, ran it for four more years, and ultimately sold the
organization."

Sue continued: "During that turnaround, Gino began developing what would become EOS. He pulled together tools and
concepts that actually worked, refining them in the trenches of
running a real business. At the same time, he became one of
the original ten members of a peer group in Detroit. In working
with the other members of that group, he discovered he had a
real knack and passion for the art and science of running a truly
great entrepreneurial company. When he sold his business, he

decided to pursue that passion full-time, continuing to refine and teach EOS."

She paused. "What he created is just a set of simple, real-world, practical tools. Timeless concepts that have been around for a hundred years and will be around for a thousand more. You're not going to find any magic pills or silver bullets in what I share with you today."

Alan felt something shift in his chest. Not hope exactly, but the absence of the cynicism he'd been carrying. This didn't sound like a sales pitch.

"Since Gino started creating EOS," Sue continued, "he and I and over one thousand other EOS Implementers around the globe have conducted tens of thousands of full-day sessions for leadership teams of tens of thousands of companies. When we work with leadership teams, we make them better at three things we call vision, traction, and healthy."

Alan noticed Karen lean forward slightly.

"Vision just means getting you 100 percent on the same page with where you're going and how you plan to get there. Traction means instilling discipline and accountability throughout your organization so that no matter where you go, you see people executing on your vision. And Healthy means making you a more cohesive, functional, open, honest, fun-loving team. Because most of the time, you're not."

Greg shifted uncomfortably in his seat. Alan noticed Karen's eyes had narrowed slightly, as if Sue had touched a nerve.

"From there, we find, as goes the leadership team, so goes the rest of the organization. The kinds of organizations we work with are entrepreneurial. Most of them have between ten and two hundred fifty employees. Their owners and leaders are growth-oriented and open-minded. They're willing to be open and honest and vulnerable with themselves and the people around them. They're more afraid of the status quo than they are of change."

Sue paused. "So that's about EOS. Now, let me share with you a little about my story."

"I've been an entrepreneur myself. Built a company, struggled with the same issues you're facing. Along the way, I discovered these tools. I started sharing them with other business owners and eventually realized that helping entrepreneurs was my true calling. I sold my company six years ago, and I've been doing this full-time ever since. I've worked with over a hundred companies. And that's why I'm excited to be here today with you, sharing EOS with you and helping you get what you want from your business."

Sue paused, allowing the weight of her story to settle over the room. The initial tension seemed to have softened; Alan was no longer glancing at the clock, and the rest of the team had stopped shifting in their seats. No one reached for a phone or looked away. Instead, they were leaning in, their focus fixed on Sue as if they were seeing their own struggles reflected in her journey. Sensing they were ready to engage, Sue turned to face the team directly.

"Now I'd like to learn a little bit about you," Sue said, turning to face the team. "Where I like to start is with a quick two-minute history. How did this whole thing start? Who can bring me up to speed?"

Alan provided the overview: fifteen years in business, staffing and recruiting firm, started in his basement, grew it to forty-five employees and eight million in revenue.

Sue asked follow-up questions, drawing responses from each person at the table. What did you do last year in revenue? What are you projecting this year? What type of business are you in? What do you do for your customers?

Then the questions got more pointed.

"Here's a question for all of you," Sue said. "What do you want from this business that you are not getting today? In other words, what's your number one business goal?"

The team members shared their answers. Growth. More control. Better margins. A leadership team that actually worked together.

"Now think about achieving that goal," Sue said. "What are the three biggest challenges? The three things that wake you up in the middle of the night when you're worrying about your business?"

Alan spoke first. "People. Finding them, keeping them, getting them to do what they're supposed to do. That's number one."

"Communication," Karen added. "We're all working on different things, and nobody knows what anyone else is doing."

"Accountability," Marcus said. "Things fall through the cracks constantly."

Greg nodded. "And we can't seem to get out of firefighting mode. Every day is a new crisis."

Sue wrote everything down, then asked: "What about your strengths? What do you do well?"

They talked about their technical expertise, their reputation in the market, their loyal customer base.

"The next three questions are going to go pretty quickly," Sue said. "I just need a number from you. Between one and ten, with ten being best. Trust your gut. Don't overthink it."

The room tensed slightly.

"How effective are your meetings? Your internal meetings with just your team."

"Three," Marcus said.

"Three," Karen agreed.

"I'd say four," Diane offered.

"Two," Greg said, surprising everyone. "Maybe two and a half. They're brutal."

Sue wrote the numbers without comment.

"Next question. How aligned is your entire organization around your vision and plan?"

Alan answered first. "Five. Maybe."

The others ranged from three to five.

"Finally, what kind of organizational accountability exists in your company? Whatever your definition of the ultimate organizational accountability is, one to ten."

"Four," Alan said quietly.

The others agreed, ranging from three to five.

Sue nodded. "Thank you for being honest. That takes courage, especially in front of each other." She looked around the table. "Is there anything I should have asked about, or anything you'd like to add that I didn't cover?"

A few shakes of the head. They'd laid it all out there.

"All right. That gives me everything I need. Let me move to step three and get into the tools with you."

Sue stood and moved to the whiteboard. "The best way for me to do this is to begin at the end. I'd like to illustrate for you what it looks like when all of our work is done."

She drew a circle in the center and wrote "Your Business" inside it.

"This model stems from a discovery: that all entrepreneurs, all entrepreneurial leaders, tend to wrestle with 136 issues simultaneously. That discovery tells us that to the extent you can strengthen the Six Key Components of your business, those 136 issues just tend to fall into place. Because they're really symptoms of the true root cause."

She drew six points around the circle: Vision, People, Data, Issues, Process, Traction.

"Those are the Six Key Components. They make up the EOS Model."

For the next thirty minutes, Sue walked through each component. She didn't use jargon or buzzwords. She spoke plainly, like a mechanic explaining what was wrong with a car.

Vision meant getting everyone 100 percent on the same page with where the organization was going and how it planned to get there. She showed them the Vision/Traction Organizer, or V/TO, an elegantly simple two-page document that answered eight questions: Core Values, Core Focus, Ten-Year Target, Marketing Strategy, 3-Year Picture, One-Year Plan, Quarterly Rocks, and Issues List.

"Most leadership teams think they're on the same page," Sue said. "But when you actually ask them to articulate the vision, you get five different answers. The V/TO eliminates that. It's yours to keep, whether you work with me or not."

People meant having the right people in the right seats. She drew a structure on the whiteboard unlike any organizational chart Alan had seen. Boxes with functions, not names. Five roles for each seat. Clear accountability.

"This is the Accountability Chart. Most org charts are historical documents. They show who reports to whom based on how things evolved over time. The Accountability Chart is different. It shows the structure your company needs to achieve its vision."

Alan thought about his revolving door of operations directors. Three in four years. Maybe the problem wasn't finding the right person. Maybe the problem was that the seat itself wasn't clearly defined.

Data meant running the business on facts and figures instead of feelings and egos. A simple Scorecard with five to fifteen numbers that gives you an absolute pulse on the business every week.

Issues meant getting really good at solving problems as they arose. Sue introduced something called IDS: Identify, Discuss, Solve.

"Most leadership teams get themselves in a room, tackle an issue, and end up discussing the heck out of it," she said, circling the word "Discuss" multiple times on the board. "Rarely do they ever identify the real root cause. Rarely do they walk out having agreed on a plan that will make the issue go away forever. We created IDS to help teams quit spinning their wheels."

Process meant documenting the handful of core processes that made the business run, then getting everyone to follow them. Consistency. Scalability.

And Traction meant bringing the vision down to the ground and executing on it with discipline and accountability. Rocks, which were ninety-day priorities. A Meeting Pulse with weekly Level 10 Meetings that would elevate their threes and fours to tens.

"We measure progress using a scale of 0 to 100 percent strong," Sue explained. "Our goal is to get you to 80 percent or better in each of the Six Key Components. One hundred percent is utopia. It's never going to happen. But 80 percent is achievable. And when you get there, everything starts to fall into place. You can grow the business to whatever size you choose. Running the company becomes more peaceful, more profitable, and more fun."

She set down her marker. "That's the model. Those are the Six Key Components. Questions so far?"

Karen leaned forward. "What's the catch?"

Sue smiled. "No catch. Just hard work. We assume you're in the right market and selling the right products or services in that market. If you're not, there's nothing we can do to help you. This is about execution. If you are in the right market, EOS will help you achieve everything you want to achieve with your business."

Sue glanced at the clock. Twenty minutes left.

"Let me share with you the process. The exact way we do what we do."

She handed each person a one-page document showing the roadmap.

"The first step is what we're doing here today, the 90-Minute Meeting. If you decide to move forward, the next step is a full day together called the Focus Day. Seven hours, give or take. In the Focus Day, we're going to work on five very important things: Hitting the Ceiling and the leadership abilities you need to break through it, your Accountability Chart, setting Rocks, your Meeting Pulse and Level 10 Meeting agenda, and a first cut at your Scorecard."

She wrote a dollar amount on the board. "Here's the way my fee works. I charge a daily fee. It's the same for every session, and it's always fully guaranteed. What that means is, at the end of every session, if you've gotten value, you hand me a check. If I don't deliver value, if I don't deliver on my promises, please don't pay me. It keeps me on my toes and helps me focus primarily on delivering value before I get anything in return."

"No contracts?" Karen asked.

"No contracts. No engagement letters. No upfront fees. You commit one session at a time."

She outlined the rest of the journey. Two Vision Building days, spaced about thirty days apart. Then, quarterly sessions to maintain momentum. Most clients stayed in the process for about two years before graduating.

"At some point, you're going to get it," Sue said. "You're going to master the process. You're going to implement the tools, and you're going to graduate. That's my job. My job isn't to dig myself deeper into the organization. My job is to help you implement these tools and then get the heck out of your way. My job is to let you run your business."

The room was quiet.

Greg spoke up. "How is this different from every other consultant we've hired?"

"I'm not a consultant," Sue said. "Consultants analyze your business and tell you what to do. I'm an Implementer. I teach, coach, and facilitate. I teach you the tools and concepts. I coach you through the hard decisions and hold you accountable when you're not doing what you said you'd do. And I facilitate your sessions so you can solve your own problems instead of depending on me for answers."

She paused. "Real change doesn't come from someone handing you answers. It comes from your team developing the discipline and skills to solve your own problems. My job is to teach you how to do that, coach you through the obstacles, then get out of your way."

Sue glanced at the clock. "We're right on schedule for 11:30. What questions do you have?"

* * *

Karen excused herself for her 11:30 call, promising to catch up with the team later.

The rest of them grabbed lunch at a restaurant near Sue's office. They were halfway through their sandwiches when Karen texted: *Call done. Joining you in 10. Don't make any decisions without me.*

By the time she arrived, Marcus and Diane had already declared themselves cautiously optimistic.

"She's different," Karen admitted as she slid into the booth. "I've never heard a consultant offer a guarantee like that. And she didn't try to sell us anything. She just explained how it works."

"The Accountability Chart made sense to me," Marcus said. "I've never really understood what I'm supposed to be accountable for versus what falls on Alan or Greg."

Diane nodded. "I liked how specific everything was. Not theoretical. Just practical tools."

Alan waited to hear from Greg, who had been unusually quiet.

"I don't know," Greg said finally. "It sounds good. But we've been burned before. How do we know this isn't just another expensive waste of time?"

"We don't," Alan said. "But Paul's brother went through it, and look at his company now. And Sue guarantees every session. If it doesn't work, we don't pay."

"What's the downside?" Karen asked.

Alan thought about it. "A few days of our time. And if it doesn't create value, we don't pay. Honestly, the downside seems pretty small compared to another year of what we've been doing."

Greg was still frowning, but Alan could see him wavering.

"I want to try it," Alan said. "I'm asking you all to commit to the Focus Day. One session. If it doesn't feel different from everything else we've tried, we walk away."

He looked around the table. One by one, they nodded.

Even Greg.

"All right," Greg said. "One session. But if this is another report full of recommendations that goes nowhere, I'm going to remind you all that I had doubts."

Alan smiled. "Fair enough."

He pulled out his phone to call Sue Hawkes and schedule the Focus Day.

For the first time in months, he felt something that resembled hope.

3

The Awakening

"Real change doesn't come from someone handing you answers."

THE FOCUS DAY was scheduled for a Tuesday three weeks after the 90-Minute Meeting. Alan had blocked the entire day and sent calendar invites to his leadership team. They'd meet at Sue's session room again. No distractions. No interruptions. Seven hours to work on the business instead of in it.

He arrived thirty minutes early and found Sue already there, setting up the room. A stack of materials sat on the table: copies of a book called *Traction* and thick three-ring binders with "Leadership Team Manual" printed on the cover, one for each team member.

"You're early," Sue said. "Good sign."

"Couldn't sleep," Alan admitted. "Kept thinking about what we're going to uncover today."

Sue smiled. "That's normal. The Focus Day has a way of making things transparent. Some leaders find that uncomfortable."

"Uncomfortable how?"

"We're going to look at your organization with fresh eyes. Structure. People. Issues. When you do that honestly, you often see things you've been avoiding." Sue set a marker on the whiteboard tray. "The question is whether you're willing to act on what you see."

Before Alan could respond, Karen walked in, followed by Marcus and Diane. Greg arrived exactly on time, which was early for him.

Greg spotted the materials and raised an eyebrow. "More reading material?"

Sue smiled. "This one you'll actually use. Every week. I promise."

"We'll see," Greg said, but he was smiling as he took his seat.

"All right," Sue said once everyone was settled. "Let's begin."

Sue started with a concept she called "Hitting the Ceiling."

"Every growing organization hits the ceiling at some point," she explained. "Revenue plateaus. Profits shrink. Problems multiply. The things that got you here won't get you to the next level."

Alan felt the words land. That was exactly where RTS had been for three years.

"To break through the ceiling," Sue continued, "leaders need to master five abilities." She wrote them on the whiteboard:

1. Simplify
2. Delegate
3. Predict
4. Systemize
5. Structure

"Most entrepreneurial companies are complex when they should be simple," Sue said. "Leaders are doing too much themselves when they should be delegating. They're reactive when they should be predicting. They lack systems and structure."

He turned to face the team. "The tools I'm going to teach you today are designed to strengthen these abilities. But here's the key: the tools only work if you actually use them. Consistently. Disciplined. Every week, every quarter, every year."

Alan wrote the five abilities in his notebook. He'd heard versions of this advice before, from books and consultants and well-meaning colleagues. But something about the way Sue presented it felt different. Simpler. More actionable.

"Let's start with Structure," Sue said. "Open your Leadership Team Manuals to the Accountability Chart section. The tool we use is called the Accountability Chart."

Sue drew a basic organizational structure on the whiteboard. Three boxes at the bottom: Sales/Marketing, Operations, Finance. A box above them labeled with an "I." A box at the very top labeled with a "V."

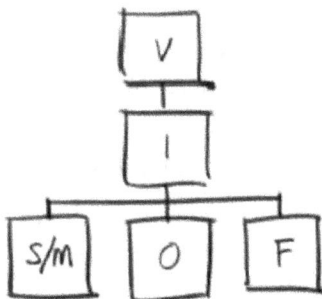

"Every organization has three major functions," Sue explained. "You have to generate leads and close sales. You have to deliver your product or service. And you have to manage the money. Those are the three boxes at the bottom."

She pointed to the "I" box. "Above them is the Integrator. This is the person who runs the day-to-day operations. The glue that holds everything together. They beat the drum, drive accountability, and integrate all the major functions so they work together harmoniously."

"That's Alan," Greg said.

"Maybe," Sue replied. "We'll see. Above the Integrator, about half the time, there's another seat called the Visionary. This is the big-picture person. The one with twenty ideas a week, nineteen of which aren't great, but one will take the company to the moon. They're creative, strategic, relationship-oriented."

Alan felt the team's eyes on him. He'd always considered himself the visionary type. Ideas came easily to him. Following through on all of them was another matter.

"Here's the problem," Sue said. "In most entrepreneurial companies, the founder is trying to fill both seats. Visionary and Integrator. That creates chaos. You get ninety-day spikes of energy and excitement, followed by periods where things fall apart because the Visionary got bored with the details."

The room went quiet. Alan recognized himself in that description.

"Let's build your Accountability Chart," Sue said. "But first, we need to figuratively fire everyone."

"Excuse me?" Karen said.

"We start with a blank slate," Sue explained. "We focus on structure first, people second. If we think about who's currently in each seat, we can't objectively determine what the right structure should be. So we pretend everyone's been fired, and we build the ideal structure for RTS. Then we figure out who belongs where."

For the next hour, the team worked through the exercise. They identified the major functions at RTS: Sales, Operations (divided into Recruiting and Client Services), and Finance. They defined five key roles for each seat, the things the person in that seat needed to obsess about and excel at.

When they finished, Sue stepped back and looked at the chart.

"Now comes the hard part," she said. "We need to put names in boxes. But before we do, I want to ask a question." She looked at Alan. "How many of these seats are you currently sitting in?"

Alan studied the Accountability Chart. The honest answer was uncomfortable.

"Three," he said slowly. "Maybe four."

"Which ones?"

"Visionary, obviously. But I'm also doing a lot of Integrator work, running the day-to-day. And I'm deeply involved in Sales." He paused. "And sometimes I jump into Operations when things go wrong."

"So four seats," Sue said. "Maybe five if we count the times you're doing Finance work that should be Karen's."

Karen shifted in her chair but didn't disagree.

"This is why you're hitting the ceiling," Sue said. "You can't do five jobs well. Nobody can. The company has grown to the point where it needs dedicated leaders in each of these seats, but you're still trying to do everything yourself."

"I know," Alan said. "I just don't know how to let go."

"That's what we're going to figure out," Sue said. "But it starts with being honest about where you are." She turned to the team. "Let's talk about who belongs in which seat. And I want us to focus on what we call GWC: Gets it, Wants it, and has the Capacity to do it. For someone to be in the right seat, they need all three."

* * *

The people conversation was harder than Alan expected.

They worked through each seat methodically. Some were easy. Karen clearly belonged in Finance. She got it, wanted it, and had the capacity. Greg belonged in Sales, despite his chronic lateness and occasional friction with other departments.

Operations was more complicated. Marcus had been running Recruiting, but when Sue pushed the team to evaluate whether he truly wanted the seat, the answer was uncertain.

"I do the job," Marcus said carefully. "I'm capable. But do I want it?" He paused. "Honestly? I'd rather be working with candidates than managing people who work with candidates."

"That's important information," Sue said. "A lot of talented people end up in leadership seats because they were good at their previous job. But managing people is a completely different skill set. And if you don't want it, you'll never be great at it."

Alan felt a knot forming in his stomach. If Marcus didn't want the Recruiting seat, who would fill it? They didn't have an obvious candidate.

"Let's put that on the Issues List," Sue said. "We'll come back to it."

The conversation about the Integrator seat was even more difficult.

"Alan, you've been functioning as the Integrator," Sue said. "But you also want to be the Visionary. You can't do both well. One of them has to go."

"I know," Alan said. "But I don't have anyone who can step into the Integrator role."

"Not yet," Sue said. "But that becomes a priority. For now, let's acknowledge the gap and put it on the Issues List. The company needs a true Integrator to reach its potential."

* * *

The rest of the Focus Day covered Rocks, the Meeting Pulse, and the Scorecard.

First came Rocks, the ninety-day priorities that would move the company forward.

"Most companies have too many priorities," Sue said. "When everything is important, nothing is important. Rocks

force you to choose. What are the three to seven most important things you need to accomplish in the next ninety days?"

At one point, during the Rocks discussion, Greg and Karen
got into a heated debate about priorities. Karen wanted to focus
on financial controls. Greg wanted to focus on sales growth.
Sue let them argue for a few minutes, then raised her hand.

"Let me ask a question," she said. "What's the one thing
that, if you accomplished it in the next ninety days, would
make the biggest impact on breaking through the ceiling?"

The room went quiet.

"If I had to pick one," Alan said slowly, "it would be solving the leadership gap in Operations. Nothing else matters if
we can't deliver on our promises to clients."

Karen and Greg both nodded. The argument dissolved.

"That's one of your Rocks," Sue said. "Now let's set all
three to seven for the company this quarter."

Next was the Meeting Pulse. A weekly 90-Minute Meeting
with a specific agenda designed to keep the team aligned and
accountable.

"This is where it all comes together," Sue said. "Same day,
same time, every week. You review your Scorecard. You check
in on Rocks. You share headlines from your week. And then
you IDS your issues: Identify, Discuss, Solve."

She walked them through the agenda, step by step. Segue.
Scorecard. Rock Review. Customer/Employee Headlines.
To-Do List. IDS. Conclude.

"Most leadership teams rate their meetings a four or five
out of ten," Sue said. "Our goal is to get you to a ten every
week. That's why we call it the Level 10 Meeting."

Finally, Sue explained the Scorecard and how to identify
five to fifteen numbers that gave them an absolute pulse on the
business every week.

"Most leadership teams fly blind," Sue said. "They don't
know if they're on track until it's too late. The Scorecard gives

you early warning signals. If a number is off track, you catch it in week one or two, not month three."

They identified key metrics: revenue, gross margin, client satisfaction scores, project completion rates, and accounts receivable aging—numbers they'd always tracked, but never systematically.

* * *

The day ended at 4:30. Alan felt simultaneously exhausted and energized.

"Homework," Sue said. "First, decide who will run your Level 10 Meetings and who will be responsible for keeping the agenda and to-do list updated. Second, schedule your first Level 10 Meeting. Put it in your calendar and hit repeat forever."

She paused. "And everyone needs to read *Traction* before our next session. It will reinforce everything we covered today."

As the team filed out, Alan hung back.

"Can I ask you something?" he said.

"Of course."

"How do you do that? The thing where you ask questions instead of giving answers? Where you let the room figure it out?"

Sue smiled. "It's called facilitation. The answer is always in the room. My job isn't to solve your problems. My job is to teach you a system and help you solve your own problems. If I just gave you answers, you'd become dependent on me. That's not what we're after."

"The answer is always in the room," Alan repeated.

"Always. The people who work in a business know more about that business than any outside consultant ever will. They just need the right tools, the right process, and the confidence to surface what they already know."

Alan tucked that phrase away. It felt important. More important than he fully understood.

* * *

Vision Building Day 1 came a month later. The team had made progress. They'd held four Level 10 Meetings, rocky at first but improving each week.

Sue led them through the first half of the V/TO, starting with Core Values.

"Core Values are the essential characteristics that define who you are as an organization," she explained. "When someone shares your Core Values, they fit your culture like a glove. When they don't, no amount of talent or experience makes up for it."

He led the team through a discovery exercise. They started by identifying people at RTS who exemplified the culture they wanted, people they'd clone if they could. Then they looked for common traits among those people.

The discussion was animated. Names flew around the room. Stories emerged about employees who went above and beyond, who embodied what RTS stood for.

After an hour of work, they had a list of five Core Values:

1. Own It (Take responsibility, no excuses)
2. Figure It Out (Resourceful problem-solving)
3. Straight Talk (Honest, direct communication)
4. Team First (Collaborate, support each other)
5. Never Settle (Continuous improvement)

"These feel right," Diane said. "This is who we are. Or who we want to be."

"Now we test them," Sue said. She directed them to a page in their Leadership Team Manuals. "This tool is called the

People Analyzer. We're going to rate every person in this room against these Core Values."

The team shifted uncomfortably, but they worked through the exercise. When Sue asked if there was anyone in the organization they were concerned about, the room went quiet.

"Tom," Karen said finally. "In Accounting."

Alan's stomach tightened. Tom had been with RTS for eight years. He was competent at his job, but something had always felt off.

The results were stark. Tom was below the bar.

"He's what we call a wrong person in the right seat," Sue said. "He can do the job, but he doesn't fit your culture. You need to have a conversation. Give him specific examples of where he's falling short. Give him a chance to change. If he can't get above the bar, you have to let him go."

Sue looked around the room. "Here's what I want you to understand. As you move forward with these tools in place, you'll only ever have two types of people issues: the right people in the wrong seat, or the wrong people in the right seat. The People Analyzer and GWC help you see which one you're dealing with and what to do about it."

Alan dreaded that conversation with Tom. But he knew Sue was right.

After Core Values, they moved to Core Focus, 10-Year Target, and Marketing Strategy. The Core Focus discussion was revelatory. Alan had always thought of RTS as a staffing company. But when Sue pushed them to articulate what they were truly passionate about, a different picture emerged.

"We don't just fill positions," Karen said. "We help businesses build teams that actually work."

"We're matchmakers," Marcus added. "We understand both sides. What companies really need, and what candidates actually want. Most staffing firms just throw resumes at job descriptions."

"That's your niche," Sue said. "You're not competing with every staffing company. You're serving business leaders who want the right people, not just warm bodies."

By the end of the day, they had a 10-Year Target that excited everyone: become the most trusted talent partner for mid-sized businesses in the Twin Cities, with fifteen million in revenue.

"That feels ambitious," Greg said.

"It should," Sue replied. "A 10-Year Target should make you a little uncomfortable. If it's easy, you're not dreaming big enough."

* * *

Vision Building Day 2 was about bringing the vision down to earth.

They completed the 3-Year Picture, the 1-Year Plan, and their first set of Quarterly Rocks. They built out the Issues List, which had grown to thirty-seven items over the past two months.

Near the end of the day, Sue asked them to rate the session.

"From one to ten," she said, "how did you do today as a team?"

"Nine," said Karen.

"Nine," said Greg.

"Nine," said Diane.

"Eight," said Marcus. "We could have been more efficient on the 3-Year Picture discussion."

"Nine," said Alan.

Sue nodded. "Good work today. You're making real progress."

The team mirrored Sue's nod and let out a collective breath of relief and accomplishment.

"You're on the journey," Sue continued. "The tools are working. But here's what I need you to understand: this is just the beginning. Implementing EOS takes about two years. You're going to have setbacks. You're going to get frustrated. There will be days when you want to give up."

She paused, and the room seemed to collectively hold its breath.

"But if you stick with it, if you trust the process and use the tools consistently, you'll look back in two years and not recognize this company. You'll be running a truly great organization. And more importantly, you'll actually enjoy doing it."

* * *

After the session, Alan helped Sue pack up the materials.

"I've been watching you," Alan said.

"Oh?"

"The way you work. You're not just facilitating sessions. You're teaching us concepts we didn't know we needed. You're coaching us through decisions we've been avoiding. And when Greg pushed back on the Accountability Chart, you didn't back down. You held him accountable. You pushed right back until he saw what he was avoiding."

Sue nodded. "That's the job. Teach, coach, facilitate. The teaching gives people tools. The facilitation helps them find their own answers. But the coaching..." She paused. "The coaching is where the real change happens. It's holding people accountable. It's having the hard conversations. It's caring enough about someone's success that you're willing to make them uncomfortable."

"Is that something you can learn? All three pieces?"

Sue looked at him with an expression Alan couldn't quite read.

"Why do you ask?"

"I don't know," Alan said. "There's something about this whole process. The tools, the system, the way it all fits together.

I find myself thinking about it constantly. Not just for RTS, but wondering how it would work for other companies."

"Interesting," Sue said. She zipped up her bag. "Let's focus on getting RTS healthy first. You've got a lot of work ahead of you."

She shook Alan's hand and headed for the door. "I'll see you at the Quarterly."

4

The Transformation

"As goes the leadership team, so goes the rest of the organization."

THE FIRST QUARTERLY session came ninety days after Vision Building Day 2. Alan wasn't sure what to expect.

"We're going to do three things today," Sue explained as the team settled into their seats. "First, we'll review where you've been. Second, we'll check in on your vision and make sure you're still aligned. Third, we'll set Rocks for the next quarter and solve some issues."

It sounded simple enough. But when Sue asked each team member to share their professional highs and lows from the past ninety days, something unexpected happened: They were honest.

Karen talked about finally getting the monthly close process under five days. Marcus admitted he still wasn't sure if he belonged in the Recruiting seat. Greg celebrated landing two new accounts but acknowledged he'd dropped the ball on follow-through with an existing client. Diane shared that she'd had three difficult conversations with underperforming employees, something she never would have done before.

And Alan reported that Tom was gone.

"The thirty-day improvement plan didn't work," Alan said. "He couldn't get above the bar. We had the conversation, gave him a fair severance, and he left two weeks ago."

"How did the rest of the organization respond?" Sue asked.

"That's the thing," Alan said. "I expected people to be upset. Tom had been here eight years. But instead, there was this collective exhale. Like everyone had been waiting for us to do something."

Sue nodded. "That's almost always what happens. The wrong people affect everyone around them. When you finally act, you're not just helping the organization. You're honoring the right people who've been carrying extra weight."

* * *

The Quarterlies became a pulse, a consistent cadence of execution that defined their new 90-Day World.

Every ninety days, the team stepped out of the business and worked on the business. This rhythm allowed them to continuously gain traction, as they reviewed their Rocks, celebrated completions, and faced the ones they'd missed. They refreshed their Scorecard numbers, watching the trends develop over thirteen weeks of data. They IDS'd through their Issues List, solving problems at the root instead of putting out the same fires over and over.

The Level 10 Meetings took time to click. The first few were awkward. People talked too long during the segue. They got stuck in the weeds on Scorecard numbers. The IDS portion devolved into circular discussions that solved nothing.

But Sue had warned them about this. "The first ten Level 10s are the hardest," she'd said. "Push through. Trust the process."

By week eight, something shifted. The meetings started ending on time. The team rated them sevens and eights instead of fours and fives. Issues that had lingered for months were finally solved. Greg, who had been the biggest skeptic, admitted he now actually looked forward to Tuesdays.

"I never thought I'd say this about a meeting," he said, "but it's the most productive ninety minutes of my week."

What surprised Alan most was the compounding effect. Each completed Rock built on the last. Each solved issue prevented three more from emerging. The weekly pulse of Level 10 Meetings created accountability that carried through the other six days.

"It's like financial compounding," Sue explained during one session. "Consistent execution, week after week, quarter after quarter. It takes you places you didn't think were possible. Most companies try to make one big leap. The ones that win make a thousand small steps in the same direction."

* * *

At the second Quarterly, they hired a true Operations leader.

Rachel Simmons came from a competitor. She'd heard about what was happening at RTS through the industry grapevine and reached out to Diane directly. Her resume was strong, but what sold Alan was her interview.

"I've been in operations my whole career," she said. "I've seen companies run well and companies run poorly. What you're building here, the discipline, the clarity, that's rare. I want to be part of it."

She got it, wanted it, and had the capacity from day one. Marcus happily moved into a senior recruiter role, relieved to be working with candidates again instead of managing people.

"I should have been more vocal about wanting to return to the recruiter role," Marcus told Alan after the transition. "I was so worried about letting you down that I stayed in a seat I hated. That wasn't fair to anyone."

"You're not letting me down," Alan said. "You're in the right seat now. That's what matters."

* * *

At the third Quarterly, revenue crossed nine million dollars.

More importantly, margins improved by three percentage points. Karen had systematized the financial controls, and the leaks were finally plugged. The Hensley Technologies relationship, which had been on life support eighteen months earlier, was now their strongest account. Bill had become a reference customer, telling anyone who would listen about RTS's transformation.

"What changed?" Bill asked Alan over lunch one day.

"We got our act together," Alan said. "Better systems. Better accountability. Better people in the right seats."

"Whatever you're doing, keep doing it. You guys used to drive me crazy. Now you're the most reliable vendor we have."

Alan thought about where they'd been just a year ago. The finger-pointing. The chaos. The feeling of drowning in his own company. It felt like a different lifetime.

The team had changed, too. They actually liked each other now. The Level 10 Meetings had created a pulse of communication that bled into everyday interactions. When issues came up, people raised them rather than letting them fester. When someone dropped a ball, the team rallied to help instead of pointing fingers.

"We're becoming a real team," Diane observed during one session. "Not just people who work in the same building."

* * *

At the fourth Quarterly, they tackled the Visionary/Integrator issue head-on.

But before they got there, there was the Two-Day Annual Planning session.

Sue had explained the Annual at Vision Building Day 2. "Once a year, you step out of the business for two full days. It's like pressing the reset button. You review everything: your V/TO, your Accountability Chart, your 3-Year Picture. You look at what worked, what didn't, and what needs to change. It's the most important session of the year."

The Two-Day Annual happened at the one-year mark. The team gathered at a retreat center outside Minneapolis, far from phones and interruptions.

Day One was about looking back and looking forward. They did the Organizational Checkup, rating the company's progress in each of the Six Key Components. The numbers surprised Alan. A year ago, they'd been fives and sixes. Now they were eights and nines. They reviewed every person in every seat, confronting the people issues that had been simmering. They refreshed the 3-Year Picture and set the 1-Year Plan.

Day Two was about execution. They set their annual Rocks, each one tied to the bigger vision. They IDSed through their major issues, going deeper than they ever could in a Quarterly session. By the end, they had a clear roadmap for the year ahead.

But what struck Alan most was the team health. This was the same group that had finger-pointed and blamed and avoided hard conversations a year ago. Now they challenged each other openly, disagreed passionately, and ultimately committed to decisions together.

"This is what healthy looks like," Sue said at the end of Day Two. "Not the absence of conflict. The ability to work through it. That's how you get real alignment."

The jump in team health from the Two-Day Annual carried through the rest of the year.

* * *

At the fourth Quarterly, Alan acknowledged what everyone already knew: he was a Visionary trapped in an Integrator's seat, and it was holding the company back.

"I need to let go of the day-to-day," Alan said. "But I don't know who can take it."

The team looked at Rachel. She'd been crushing it in Operations. She was organized and disciplined, and she had a gift for holding people accountable without creating resentment. In Level 10 Meetings, she kept discussions on track and called out when they were spinning rather than solving.

"Would you want it?" Alan asked her.

Rachel didn't hesitate. "Yes. I've been thinking about it for months. I didn't want to overstep, but I know I can do this."

The transition took ninety days. Sue coached them through it, helping Alan let go of responsibilities he'd held for fifteen years and helping Rachel step into authority she'd never had before. They promoted Kevin, one of Rachel's direct reports, into the Operations seat. He was young but hungry, and Rachel had been preparing him for the position without realizing it.

There were bumps. Alan caught himself jumping into operational issues more than once. Rachel had to learn to push back when he did. Kevin stumbled early, overwhelmed by the scope of his new role, but Rachel coached him through it, just as Sue had coached her.

* * *

By the fifth Quarterly, the reorganization was working. Rachel was the Integrator. Kevin was running Operations. Alan had finally let go.

He came to the office three days a week instead of six. He focused on strategy, relationships, and the handful of big ideas that could take RTS to the next level. The company didn't fall apart. If anything, it ran better without him in the middle of everything.

Revenue hit ten million dollars that quarter. They'd grown more in fifteen months than in the previous three years combined.

"Turns out I was the bottleneck," Alan admitted to Sarah one night. "All those years, I thought I was the only one who could do things right. I was actually the one slowing everything down."

* * *

The changes at work were significant. But the changes at home were what surprised Alan most.

He made it to his daughter, Emily's, soccer games. Not some of them. All of them. He sat in the bleachers with Sarah, cheering and groaning and feeling the sun on his face, and he realized he'd missed years of this.

He took vacations. Real vacations, where he left his laptop at home and didn't check his email. The first one was terrifying. He spent the first two days convinced the company was imploding without him. By day three, he'd finally relaxed. By day seven, he didn't want to go back.

"You're different," Sarah said one evening after a game. Emily had scored twice, and they'd taken her out for ice cream to celebrate.

"Different how?"

"Calmer. More present." She paused. "You used to be here, but not here, you know? Always thinking about work. Now you're actually with us."

Alan didn't know what to say. She was right. For fifteen years, he'd carried the business everywhere. In bed at night, at the dinner table, on vacation. It had been a constant weight, a hum of anxiety that never fully quieted.

Now the hum was gone. Not because he cared less about RTS, but because the business was finally running without him having to touch everything. The system worked. The team worked. He could step away and trust that things wouldn't fall apart.

He was sleeping through the night for the first time in years.

* * *

At the eighth Quarterly, two years into the journey, Sue made an announcement.

"I have some news," she said after they'd completed the check-in. "You're ready to graduate."

The room went quiet.

"What do you mean?" Karen asked.

"I mean, you don't need me anymore," Sue said, smiling. "That was always the goal. I told you in our first session that my job is to work myself out of a job. You've implemented the system. You're running Level 10 Meetings without me. You're solving your own issues. You've mastered EOS."

The room was quiet. Alan felt something shift in his chest.

"That's the average, by the way," Sue continued. "Two years. Most clients graduate around this point. Some graduate and never look back. Others find value in continuing with an outside perspective, someone to keep them accountable and challenge their thinking."

She paused. "I should also mention that I'm transitioning to Emeritus status with EOS Worldwide. After seventeen years, I'm scaling back to just four to six clients. But that's not why I'm raising graduation. I'm raising it because you've earned it. You're ready."

"I vote we keep you," Greg said immediately. "You're the only one who tells me when I'm being an idiot."

The team laughed. Karen and Rachel nodded their agreement.

"We want to continue," Alan said. "You've earned your place in this room."

"Then I'd be honored to stay," Sue said. "I'm moving to Arizona, but I'll fly back for sessions. You're one of the teams I'm not ready to say goodbye to."

* * *

Year three was when everything clicked.

Revenue hit twelve million. They'd added eight employees, all carefully vetted against the Core Values before being hired. The Level 10 Meetings ran like clockwork, with team members rotating as the facilitator because they'd all learned how. Client satisfaction scores were the highest in company history.

Alan found himself doing something he'd never done before: turning down work.

"We can't be everything to everyone," Rachel reminded him when a large prospect came calling with a project that didn't fit their Core Focus. "We're not a temp agency. We're talent partners for mid-sized businesses. This project is outside our sweet spot."

She was right. They passed on the opportunity, and three months later they landed a client who fit perfectly. The discipline was paying off.

* * *

Year four brought new challenges. Two competitors merged, creating a larger player in the market. A key employee left to start his own firm. The economy wobbled, and two clients froze their hiring budgets.

But the team handled it. The issues were added to the list, IDS'd, and resolved. The Scorecard showed the dips early, giving them time to respond. The Rocks kept them focused on what mattered most instead of panicking about everything.

"Three years ago, any one of these would have sent us into a tailspin," Karen observed at a Quarterly. "Now they're just issues to solve."

Revenue dipped slightly that year, to eleven-five. But profits actually increased because they'd built enough margin into the business to weather storms. By year five, they were back on track and growing again.

* * *

Year five was when the calls started coming.

First, it was a private equity firm, sniffing around mid-sized staffing companies in the Midwest. Then, a larger competitor looking to expand its geographic footprint. Then, a strategic buyer, an HR services company that wanted to add a recruiting arm.

"Are you interested in selling?" they all asked.

Alan's first instinct was to say no. RTS was his baby. He'd built it from nothing. The thought of handing it over to strangers felt like betrayal.

But Sarah asked a question that stuck with him.

"What do you want to be doing in five years?"

He didn't have a good answer. Running RTS, he supposed. Growing it bigger. But when he imagined himself at sixty, still in the same office, still solving the same types of problems, something felt off.

He talked to Sue about it during their next session.

"It's a question every entrepreneur eventually faces," Sue said. "You've built something valuable. You've proven you can run it well. The question is whether running it is still what you want to do."

"I don't know," Alan admitted. "I love the team. I love what we've built. But lately I've been feeling restless. Like there's something else I'm supposed to be doing."

Sue smiled. "That restlessness is data. Pay attention to it."

* * *

Year six, RTS hit fifteen million in revenue.

Fifty-two employees. Margins that made Karen smile every month. A leadership team that could run the company without Alan being in the building. They'd achieved everything they'd put on the V/TO five years earlier, and then some.

The acquisition offers kept coming. Alan had been brushing them off for a year, but something had shifted. The restlessness he talked about with Sue wasn't going away. If anything, it was growing stronger.

He and Sarah talked about it over several long dinners. What did they want the next chapter to look like? What would give Alan the sense of purpose he was craving? The financial security from a sale would open doors. The question was which door he wanted to walk through.

Alan engaged a business broker, someone Sue recommended who understood EOS companies. They ran a formal process, entertaining offers from three serious buyers. The numbers were bigger than Alan had ever imagined.

"You've built something special," the broker told him. "Buyers pay a premium for companies that run themselves. Most businesses this size are completely dependent on the founder. RTS isn't. That's rare, and it's valuable."

Over three months, Alan and Rachel met with each prospective buyer. They toured facilities, reviewed integration plans, and asked hard questions about culture and people. Alan wasn't just selling a company; he was entrusting his team to new owners. That mattered more than the price.

The winning offer came from a regional staffing firm looking to expand into the Twin Cities. They wanted to keep the RTS brand, keep the team, and keep the culture. Rachel would become president. The integration would be gradual and respectful.

Alan negotiated hard, not just on price but on terms. He wanted protection for his employees, guarantees that the Core Values would be honored, and commitments that the EOS system would continue to be upheld. The buyers agreed to everything.

The deal closed on a Tuesday in October, six years after Alan had first walked into Sue Hawkes's office for a 90-Minute Meeting. Six years since he'd learned about Hitting the Ceiling and The Accountability Chart and the power of ninety-day Rocks.

Alan deposited a check larger than he'd ever dreamed of. He'd started RTS with a credit card and a prayer. He was leaving it with financial security for the rest of his life.

* * *

The transition took ninety days. Alan stayed on as a consultant, helping Rachel and the new owners navigate the integration. But increasingly, his presence wasn't needed. The systems worked. The team was strong. RTS would be fine without him.

His last day was a Friday in January. The team threw him a party in the conference room where they'd held hundreds of Level 10 Meetings. There were speeches and toasts and a gift:

a framed copy of their original V/TO from Vision Building Day 2, now covered with checkmarks and completion dates.

"You changed our lives," Rachel told him. "Not just the business. Our lives. We're better leaders, better people, because of what you built here."

Alan couldn't speak for a moment. He looked around the room at faces he'd worked alongside for years. Karen, still sharp as ever. Greg, who'd gone from skeptic to true believer. Diane, who'd found her voice and become indispensable. Rachel, who'd grown from Operations manager to president.

"I didn't do it alone," he finally said. "This team did it. I just got us pointed in the right direction."

After the last handshake, after the conference room emptied and the leftover cake was wrapped in plastic, Alan walked through the building one final time.

The recruiting floor, where he'd spent countless nights reviewing resumes and calling candidates in the early years. Karen's office, where they'd sweated over cash flow projections that had seemed insurmountable at the time. The break room where he'd announced the first big contract, the one that had made everything possible.

Fifteen years of his life were embedded in these walls. Every triumph. Every failure. Every lesson that had shaped him into someone capable of walking away.

He paused at the front door, his hand on the handle.

"Thank you," he said quietly to the empty building. Then he stepped outside and didn't look back.

* * *

The drive home that night was quiet. Sarah was waiting with two cups of hot tea and a question.

"So what now?"

Alan had been thinking about that for months. He had more money than he'd ever need. He was fifty-two years old, healthy, energetic, with decades of productive years ahead of him. He could retire, but the thought made him restless. He could start another company, but that didn't excite him either.

What excited him was something else entirely.

"I keep thinking about Sue," Alan said. "About what she did for us. For me. She walked into a broken company and helped us fix it. Not by telling us what to do, but by teaching us a system, coaching us through the hard parts, and holding us accountable when we wanted to take shortcuts."

Sarah nodded. She knew where this was going.

"Remember when she called me out for micromanaging Rachel? Or when she pushed Greg to finally have that conversation with his underperformer?" Alan shook his head. "That's the part that made the difference. Not just the tools. The coaching. Someone willing to tell us the truth, even when we didn't want to hear it.

"I want to do that for other people," Alan decided. "I want to help entrepreneurs the way Sue helped me."

"You want to become an EOS Implementer."

"I think so. I know it sounds crazy. I just spent twenty-one years building a company, and now I want to start over in a completely different career."

Sarah took his hand. "It doesn't sound crazy. It sounds like you."

* * *

The next morning, Alan called Sue Hawkes in Arizona.

"I want to do what you do," Alan said. "I want to become an EOS Implementer. What do I need to know?"

Sue paused. "That's a significant decision. What's driving this?"

"I've been thinking about it since I first watched you facilitate," Alan said. "The way you helped us see what we couldn't see ourselves. I want to learn how to do that for other people."

"So you've been sitting with this for a while."

"Remember when you told me to get RTS in shape before I considered what you do? Well, it's been that long."

Sue was quiet for a moment. "I can tell you about the path. There's a training program called Boot Camp for people who want to do this work. But Alan, I need to be honest about something first."

"What's that?"

"This isn't a job. It's a calling. The training is intense. Building a practice takes years. You'll face rejection and doubt and moments when you wonder what you've gotten yourself into." Sue paused. "But if you have the passion for it, if you genuinely want to help entrepreneurs get what they want from their businesses, there's nothing more rewarding. I've been doing this for eighteen years, and I still can't believe I get paid to do work this meaningful."

Alan felt something settle in his chest. A certainty he hadn't felt since the early days of RTS, when everything was possible, and the future was wide open.

"Tell me more," he said.

5

The Seed

*"Passion can't be manufactured.
Either you have it, or you don't."*

THREE WEEKS HAD passed since Alan's final day at RTS. Three weeks of quiet mornings and unhurried afternoons. Three weeks of realizing that, for the first time in twenty-one years, no one needed him to solve anything.

The freedom should have felt liberating. Instead, it felt like free fall.

When Sue agreed to fly back to Minneapolis to talk in person, Alan felt something settle. A direction, finally. A next step.

They met at a coffee shop near Sue's old office. Sue had flown in from Arizona specifically for this conversation.

"Some conversations need to happen face to face," Sue had said. "This is one of them."

Sue was already seated when Alan arrived, a cup of black coffee in front of her. She looked relaxed and tanned, the Arizona sun agreeing with her. No whiteboard, no agenda, no leadership team waiting to be facilitated. Just two people having coffee.

The espresso machine hissed in the background, punctuating their conversation with bursts of steam.

"Thanks for flying back," Alan said, sliding into the booth across from her.

"Of course. This is important." Sue smiled. "You've been thinking about this for years now. Since that first question you asked about facilitation. It's time we talked seriously."

Alan didn't respond. He wasn't sure what to say. Three weeks ago, he'd been Visionary and CEO of a company. Now he was something else entirely. Someone with resources and time and a restless feeling that wouldn't go away.

"So," Sue said, "you want to know what this life is really like."

Alan started with the obvious question. "You've been doing this for eighteen years now. Is it still what you thought it would be?"

Sue leaned back. "It's more. Much more. I've worked with over a hundred companies. That's hundreds of entrepreneurs whose lives are different because of what we did together. Thousands of employees who work in healthier organizations. Families that are stronger because a business owner finally has time and energy for them."

"That's what you said when I asked about it years ago. The impact."

"Because it's the only thing that matters. The money is nice, the freedom is wonderful, but the impact is why you get up in the morning." Sue took a sip of coffee. "Let me tell you something I've never told you before. When I first became an Implementer, I thought it was about business. Helping companies run better. And it is that. But it's really about people. It's about watching someone transform from frustrated and overwhelmed to confident and free. It's about seeing a marriage heal because a spouse finally comes home with energy instead of exhaustion."

Alan nodded. He'd experienced that himself. The way EOS had changed not just RTS but also his relationship with Sarah and his presence with Emily.

74

"That's what hooked me," Sue said. "And it's what will hook you, if you do this."

"What's it actually like? The day-to-day?"

"I work with about twenty active clients. Sometimes a few more, sometimes a few less. I see each team about five times per year. Focus Day, two Vision Building Days, then Quarterlies and Annuals. Over a two-year period, that's roughly ten sessions. After two years, about eighty percent graduate. They've mastered the system and don't need me anymore. That's the goal."

She paused. "Actually, I should clarify. That's what my practice looked like when I was full-time. After my transition, I only have around four to six clients, but twenty is the sweet spot for most Implementers."

"And the other twenty percent?"

"A handful stay on longer. I have some clients who've been with me from the very beginning, eighteen years now. They find value in having an outside perspective, someone to keep them sharp. And honestly, a handful never make it to graduation. They quit early, or they're not truly committed to the work." She shrugged. "That's the reality. Not everyone is ready."

"That doesn't sound like a full schedule."

"It's not, by design." Sue smiled. "Let me break down the math for you. I do about a hundred sessions per year. Each session is a full day, so that's a hundred working days. I spend another fifty to sixty days on business development. Building relationships, giving talks, and staying connected to my referral network. And I spend fifty to sixty days practicing my craft, studying the tools, and sharpening my skills as a teacher, facilitator, and coach. Mastery requires constant attention."

"So that's what, two hundred and twenty days?"

"Give or take. Which means I take about a hundred and fifty days off per year. Real days off. Not working, not thinking about work. Golf, grandkids, travel, whatever I want." Sue leaned back. "When I was full-time, I made more money than I ever made running my own company. Significantly more."

Alan raised an eyebrow. "Really?"

"The business model is elegant. No employees, no overhead, no inventory. Just you and your expertise. Once you build your client base, the economics are remarkable."

"How long does that take? Building the client base?"

"The system is designed for you to have twenty clients within about three years. That's the sweet spot. Twenty clients, roughly a hundred sessions per year. New Implementers charge around four thousand dollars per session. Do the math: a hundred sessions at four thousand each is four hundred thousand dollars a year, with a hundred and fifty days off. We call it the four-hundred-thousand-dollar system."

Alan let that sink in. Four hundred thousand dollars. A hundred and fifty days off. Twenty companies transformed.

"And as you grow," Sue continued, "your fees grow with you. Experienced Implementers charge around eight thousand per session. Same hundred sessions, but the economics get even better. That's how I made more than I ever did running my own company, while working far fewer days."

"But it's not about the money," Sue quickly added. "I mean, the money is nice. It creates freedom. But the real reward is the impact. But the real reward is seeing that freedom ripple outward—from the leadership team to their employees, and ultimately back to their families. Once you see a business owner finally show up for their family because the business is healthy, you can't walk away from this work."

She leaned forward. "That's why I call it a life sentence. Once you've experienced that kind of impact, you can't walk away. You don't want to."

Alan was quiet for a long moment. The coffee shop buzzed around them, but he barely noticed.

"Why are you telling me all this?" he finally asked.

"Because you asked," Sue said simply. "You called me. You flew me back here. You're the one pursuing this."

"But do you think I could actually do it?"

Sue set down her cup. "That's not my question to answer. Plenty of successful entrepreneurs could do this work. The question is whether you're called to it. Whether you'll wake up excited to do it. Whether it's what you're meant to do with this next chapter of your life."

She leaned back. "I can tell you about the path, the economics, the community. But I can't tell you if this is right for you. Only you know that."

Alan felt something settle in his chest. Not an endorsement. Not recruitment. Just information. The decision was entirely his.

Alan shook his head. "I just finished one chapter. I'm not sure I'm ready to start another."

"That's fair," Sue said. "But you've already sold RTS. You're effectively retired. The question isn't whether you have time. The question is what you want to do with it."

Alan considered that. She was right. He'd built something that didn't need him anymore. Now he was free. And freedom, he was discovering, came with its own challenges.

"I'm fifty-two years old," Alan said. "Isn't it a little late to start a new career?"

"That's another question you'll have to answer for yourself," Sue said. "I can tell you that most Implementers come to this in their late forties to early sixties. You need the experience, the scar tissue, the wisdom that only comes from building something yourself. But whether fifty-two is the right age for you? That's your call."

* * *

They talked for another hour. Sue explained the path: the application process, the training at Boot Camp, and the first year of building a practice. She talked about the community of Implementers, hundreds of people around the world doing the same work, supporting each other, sharing best practices.

"It's a franchise," Sue said. "You're expected to follow the proven system. EOS works because it's delivered the same way, every time, by every Implementer. That consistency is what creates results. But within that structure, you're building your own practice, your own client relationships. And you're never alone. The community is always there."

"Tell me more about the community."

"It's one of the things that surprised me most," Sue said. "When I started, I expected competition. Scarcity. People protecting their territory. That's how most industries work. But EOS is different. The mindset is abundance. Help first, always."

"Help first?"

"If another Implementer needs advice, you give it freely. If they're struggling with a client situation, you share what you've learned. If they're in your city and need a referral, you send it their way." Sue shook her head. "I know it sounds idealistic. But it's real. I've experienced it hundreds of times. Implementers genuinely want each other to succeed."

"Why?"

"Because we believe there's more than enough work for everyone. There are millions of entrepreneurial companies in the world. Millions of leadership teams that need help. The problem isn't competition for clients. The problem is reaching all the companies that are struggling and don't know help exists."

Alan thought about the entrepreneurs he knew. Friends from his Roundtable. Vendors. Clients. Most of them were grinding through the same frustrations he'd experienced before EOS. They didn't know a better way was possible.

"There's also accountability," Sue continued. "We meet in small groups called T-Groups. Three to five Implementers who challenge each other, support each other, and hold each other to our standards. Iron sharpens iron. You become better because you're surrounded by people who won't let you coast."

"What's the hardest part?"

Sue considered the question. "The first year. You're learning to facilitate instead of consult. You're building your client base from scratch. You're developing confidence in the room. It's humbling. You'll make mistakes. You'll have sessions that don't go well. You'll doubt yourself."

"That sounds terrible."

"It is, sometimes. But it's also exhilarating. And here's what I've learned: the struggle is the point. It's what teaches you. The Implementers who skip the struggle, who try to short-cut the process, never develop real mastery. The ones who embrace it, who stay humble and keep learning, they become great."

Alan nodded slowly. He thought about his own journey with EOS. The early skepticism. The awkward first Level 10 Meetings. The difficult conversation with Tom. None of it had been easy. But all of it had been worth it.

"You've already taken the hardest step," Sue said. "Letting go of RTS. Most entrepreneurs never manage that. They stay attached forever, even when the business no longer needs them. You built something valuable, grew it, and had the wisdom to hand it off. That takes courage."

"It didn't feel like courage. It felt like the right time."

"That's what courage feels like when you're living it."

* * *

Alan drove home in silence, Sue's words echoing in his head.

Sarah was in the kitchen when he walked in, preparing dinner. She looked up and smiled.

"How was it? What did Sue say?"

"A lot." Alan sat down at the kitchen table. He told her about the conversation. The daily reality of an Implementer's life. The economics. The community. The path forward.

Sarah listened without interrupting. When he finished, she nodded slowly.

"You already decided, didn't you? Before you even met with her today."

Alan paused. She was right. He'd decided the moment he'd called Sue from the car on his last day at RTS. Maybe even before that. Maybe the decision had been forming for years, ever since he'd first watched Sue facilitate and thought, *I want to learn how to do that.*

"I think I did," he admitted. "I just needed to hear it out loud. To make sure it was real."

"It's real." Sarah reached across the table and took his hand. "I've watched you for the past six years, Alan. I've seen you transform from someone drowning to someone thriving. And I've seen how much you love talking about EOS, how you light up when you're helping other entrepreneurs understand what's possible."

"You don't think I'm crazy? Starting over at fifty-two?"

"I think you'd be crazy not to. You have a chance to spend the next twenty years doing something that matters to you, something that helps people. How many people get that chance?"

* * *

Over the following weeks, Alan dove deeper.

He reread *Traction*, this time with different eyes. Not as a client implementing the system, but as someone studying how to teach it. He noticed things he'd missed before. The structure of the tools. The sequence of the process. The philosophy underneath.

He bought *Rocket Fuel* and read it in two days. The description of the Visionary/Integrator relationship felt like reading his own story with Rachel. Then, *Get a Grip*, a business fable that followed a leadership team through their EOS journey. He recognized himself in the characters, their struggles, and their breakthroughs.

Then, *How to Be a Great Boss*, *What the Heck Is EOS?*, and everything else in the Traction Library. He devoured them all, taking notes, highlighting passages, connecting ideas.

He started noticing EOS everywhere. A friend mentioned they'd hired an Implementer. A podcast guest referenced The Accountability Chart. An article about successful companies quoted Gino Wickman. It was like learning a new word and suddenly hearing it in every conversation.

He visited Rachel at RTS one afternoon and watched her facilitate a Level 10 Meeting from the back of the room. She was good. Really good. She'd internalized the system so deeply that it had become invisible, just the way they worked. That was the goal. That was mastery.

I helped build that, Alan thought. *I can help build it elsewhere.*

At night, after Sarah went to bed, he found himself on the EOS Worldwide website. Reading about the Implementer community. Watching videos of Mark O'Donnell explaining the mission.

What struck Alan was Mark's background. He was the current Visionary at EOS Worldwide, but he'd worn every hat in the EOS world. He'd been a client who used an EOS Implementer to transform his own company. He'd been a Self-Implementer, running his business on EOS without outside help. He'd become a practicing EOS Implementer himself, then a Coach helping new Implementers find their footing, then Head Coach overseeing the entire coaching program. Now he led the organization as Visionary while still maintaining his own Implementer practice.

He'd lived every step of the journey Alan was considering. That meant something.

Alan found himself looking at the faces of Implementers from around the world. They looked happy. Fulfilled. Like people who had found their thing.

One night, he found a button that said "Become an Implementer."

He clicked.

6

The Call

"Skills can be taught. Values can't."

THE EMAIL ARRIVED shortly after Alan clicked the button.

Thank you for your interest in becoming an EOS Implementer. We'd like to schedule a call to learn more about you and share more about us. Please use the link below to find a time that works.

Simple. Professional. No hard sell. Alan liked that.

He scheduled the call for the following Tuesday at 2 p.m., blocking two hours on his calendar even though the email said to expect sixty to ninety minutes. He wanted space to think afterward.

The days leading up to the call felt strange. He found himself rehearsing what he'd say, then reminding himself this wasn't a job interview. Or was it? He genuinely didn't know what to expect.

He told Sarah about it over dinner.

"What do you think they'll ask?" she said.

"I have no idea. Sue said there's a process, but she didn't give me details."

"Are you nervous?"

Alan considered the question. "A little. It's been a long time since I've been evaluated by anyone. When you run your own company, nobody tells you if you're doing it right. You just figure it out."

"Maybe that's part of the appeal," Sarah said. "Being part of something bigger. Having standards to meet."

She was right, Alan realized. Part of what drew him to this was exactly that: the chance to be held to a higher standard, to be part of a community that cared about excellence.

* * *

At 1:55 p.m. on Tuesday, Alan sat in his home office with a fresh cup of coffee and a legal pad. He'd written notes about his background, his experience with EOS, and his reasons for wanting to become an Implementer. It felt like preparing for an important client meeting, except he was the one being evaluated.

His phone rang at exactly 2:00.

"Alan? This is Lauren Shaver from EOS Worldwide. Is now still a good time?"

"It is. Thanks for calling."

"Of course. I've been looking forward to this." Her voice was warm but direct. No small talk, no wasted words. "I've reviewed your application, and I'd love to hear more. Let's start with the big question: Why do you want to be an EOS Implementer?"

Alan had prepared for this. He talked about his experience as a client. The transformation at RTS. The way the tools had changed not just his business but his life. He talked about Sue Hawkes, watching her facilitate, the moment he realized there was something special about this work.

"I've built companies," Alan said. "I've made money. But I've never felt the kind of fulfillment I saw in Sue. She's genuinely happy. Not just successful, but fulfilled. I want that."

Lauren was quiet for a moment. "That's a good answer. Better than most. But I need to push a little deeper. Is this about the lifestyle? The money? The freedom? Or is it about something else?"

Alan paused. The honest answer was complicated. "It's all of those things," he admitted. "But if I'm being completely honest, the thing that keeps pulling me is the impact. I've watched entrepreneurs struggle my whole career. Friends, colleagues, vendors. They're grinding themselves into the ground, and they don't know there's a better way. I want to show them."

"Good," Lauren said. "Now let's talk about what it actually takes. There are five key ingredients we look for in every Implementer candidate. I want to walk through each of them with you."

Alan nodded, the weight of the moment settling in. He reached for his pen and turned the page of his notebook to a clean, white sheet, ready to capture what came next. The shift in his focus was clear; he wasn't just listening anymore—he was preparing to learn.

"The first ingredient is Passion," Lauren said. "Not interest. Not curiosity. Passion. A genuine fire for helping entrepreneurs get what they want from their businesses. This work is hard. You'll have sessions that don't go well. Clients who resist. Days when you question everything. The only thing that gets you through is passion for the mission."

"I understand," Alan said.

"Do you? Because here's what I've learned: passion can't be manufactured. Either you have it, or you don't. And the only way to know if you have it is to be honest with yourself." She paused. "So tell me: Is this a passion? Or is this just an interesting opportunity?"

Alan thought about the nights he'd spent reading the Traction Library. The conversations with Sarah. The way he'd watched Rachel facilitate Level 10 Meetings, studying her technique like a student. The way he couldn't stop thinking about this.

"It's a passion," he said. "I've started a lot of things in my life. Built companies, launched products, chased opportunities. This feels different. This feels like something I'm supposed to do."

"Good. Let's move to the second ingredient: Purity."

Alan leaned back, absorbing the weight of the word Lauren had just spoken: *Purity*. He looked down at his notes, where the word *Passion* stood alone at the top of the page. He knew what was coming next would challenge his instincts as a founder, and he steeled himself to listen with an open mind, his pen hovering just above the paper in anticipation.

"EOS works because it's delivered purely," Lauren explained. "The same tools, the same sequence, the same methodology. Every time, by every Implementer. When clients get EOS in its purest form, they get results. When Implementers start bolting on their own ideas, adding their own frameworks, mixing in other methodologies, the results suffer."

Alan felt something tighten in his chest. He had ideas. Lots of them. Twenty-one years of running a company had given him opinions about leadership, strategy, and management. Was he supposed to abandon all of that?

"I can hear you thinking," Lauren said. "Let me guess: you have your own ideas. Things you've learned. Approaches that have worked for you."

"Yes."

"And you're wondering if you have to throw all of that away to become an Implementer."

"Honestly? Yes."

Lauren laughed softly. "You don't have to throw it away. But you do have to set it aside when you're in the room. EOS is a complete system. It doesn't need additions or improvements. Your job as an Implementer is to deliver EOS purely, to trust that the system works, and to resist the temptation to bolt on your own stuff."

"Why is that so important?"

"Because the moment you start adding to EOS, you're no longer implementing EOS. You're implementing your own hybrid system. And your hybrid system hasn't been tested on tens of thousands of companies. EOS has. Purity is what protects the client."

Alan wrote the word *Purity* on his legal pad and underlined it twice.

"This is where most people struggle," Lauren continued. "Experienced entrepreneurs, successful executives, people who've achieved a lot. They come into this thinking their experience is their greatest asset. And it is, in some ways. But it can also be their greatest liability if they can't set it aside and trust the system."

"How do I know if I can do that?"

"You sit with it. You ask yourself: Am I willing to be a student again? Am I willing to follow a proven process, even when I think I know a better way? Am I humble enough to trust something bigger than my own experience?" She paused. "Those aren't easy questions. Take your time with them."

During Lauren's pause, Alan began considering her questions, jotting them down on a new sheet of paper to address after the call.

"The third ingredient is Story," Lauren said. "Every great Implementer has a compelling entrepreneurial story. They've built something. They've struggled. They've hit the ceiling and broken through it. That story is what gives them credibility in the room."

"I've definitely struggled," Alan said with a chuckle.

"Tell me about it."

Alan told her more about RTS. The early years of growth, then the plateau. The frustration, the sleepless nights, the feeling of drowning in his own company. He told her about discovering EOS, the transformation, the moment he realized he'd built something that didn't need him anymore.

"That's a powerful story," Lauren said. "The best Implementers can connect their story to their clients' pain. When you're sitting across from a frustrated entrepreneur, you can look them in the eye and say, 'I've been where you are. I know what this feels like. And I know the way out.' That's what Story gives you."

"Sue did that with me," Alan said, remembering their first 90-Minute Meeting. "She said she'd built a company and transformed it with EOS. It made everything she said more credible."

"Exactly. Story isn't just background. It's connection."

Alan nodded as Lauren continued.

"The fourth ingredient is Network," Lauren said. "When you become an Implementer, you're building a business from scratch. You need clients. And the fastest way to get clients is through relationships you already have."

"I've been in Minneapolis for thirty years," Alan said. "I know a lot of people."

"Tell me about your network."

Alan talked about his Business Roundtable. His industry contacts. Vendors and clients he'd worked with for over two decades. Friends who ran businesses, colleagues who'd moved to other companies, connections he'd made through community involvement.

"That's a strong foundation," Lauren said. "We call it your 'backyard.' The geographic area where you have a density of relationships. The most successful Implementers build their entire practice in their backyard. Twenty clients, all within driving distance. That's the goal."

"Is there a minimum? A certain number of connections I need?"

"No formula. But the more relationships you have, the faster you can build. And remember, this is a referral-based business. One great client leads to two more. Two leads to four. Your network is the seed, but the referrals are what make it grow."

The names of people Alan could help began appearing in his mind.

"The fifth ingredient is Emotional Intelligence," Lauren said. "This might be the most important one, and it's the hardest to teach."

"What do you mean by emotional intelligence in this context?"

"Can you read a room? Can you sense when someone's holding back, when there's tension below the surface, when the real issue isn't being discussed? Can you sit in uncomfortable silence and let it do its work? Can you enter the danger, call out what no one else will name, and do it with compassion instead of judgment?"

Alan thought about the sessions he'd been through with Sue. The moments when Sue had said the thing no one wanted to hear. The way she'd done it without making people defensive. The way silence had sometimes been the most powerful tool in the room.

"I think I can," Alan said. "But I've never done it professionally."

"That's honest. And it's the right answer. Emotional intelligence can be developed, but it has to start with self-awareness. The fact that you're not overconfident tells me something good."

That was a lot for Alan to think about after this call.

"Those are the five ingredients," Lauren said. "Passion, Purity, Story, Network, and Emotional Intelligence. You need all five to succeed as an Implementer."

"What if someone is weak in one area?"

"Good question. The reality is, if you're weak in one or two ingredients, you can sometimes overcome that with an over-abundance in another. For example, if your network is thin, you can compensate with extraordinary passion and hustle. If your story isn't as strong, exceptional emotional intelligence can help you connect with clients in other ways. But you can't be missing an ingredient entirely. And the stronger you are across all five, the faster you'll build your practice."

"How do you evaluate them? Is there a test?"

"There's a process. First, you'll go through a community assessment. Members of our Implementer community will meet you, talk with you, and evaluate whether you have what it takes. They have to approve you before you can move forward."

Alan felt the weight of that. It wasn't just EOS Worldwide making a decision. The community itself decided who belonged.

"Why does the community have approval?" he asked.

"Because we protect our culture fiercely. Every person we let in affects everyone else. If someone joins who doesn't share our values, who isn't EOS Pure, or who has a scarcity mindset, they contaminate the whole community. So we're careful. Very careful."

"What percentage of candidates make it through?"

"Most who get to this stage make it. We do a lot of filtering before that point. But some don't. And that's okay. This work isn't for everyone. It's better to find that out early than to strug-gle for years in the wrong calling."

"And if the community approves me?"

"Then you go to Boot Camp. Three days of intensive train-ing on how to implement EOS. Once you're at Boot Camp, you're in. You're part of the community. That's when the real journey begins."

The call lasted ninety minutes. By the end, Alan felt ener-gized and sobered at the same time.

"What happens next?" he asked.

"I'll send you information about the community assessment. You'll meet with some of our Implementers. They'll get to know you, and you'll get to know them. If they approve you, we'll schedule your Boot Camp. In the meantime, I want you to sit with everything we discussed. Especially Purity. That's where experienced entrepreneurs usually face their biggest challenge."

"Sue told me the same thing."

"Sue's wise. Listen to her." Lauren paused. "One more thing, Alan. I want you to understand something about this community. In my years of business, I've been part of peer groups, networking organizations, and industry associations. I've never experienced anything like what we have here."

"Everyone says that about their community," Alan said.

"They do. And I understand your skepticism. But I'm telling you the truth. The abundance mindset is real. The Help First mentality is real. People genuinely want each other to succeed." She paused. "When you experience your first QCE, the Quarterly Collaborative Exchange, where all the Implementers come together, when you see a hundred Implementers genuinely celebrating each other's wins, you'll understand. There's nothing like this community anywhere in the business world."

Alan wasn't sure what to make of that. He'd heard similar claims before. But something in Lauren's voice told him she believed it completely.

"This isn't a decision to make lightly," Lauren continued. "Becoming an Implementer means burning the boats. You can't do this halfway. You can't keep one foot in your old life and one foot in this new one. If you're going to do it, you have to fully commit."

"I've already sold my company," Alan said. "So the boats are already burned, in a sense."

"That helps," Lauren said. "Some candidates struggle because they're trying to hold onto their business while building an Implementer practice. But the principle still applies. Even without a company to run, you'll have to commit fully. No side consulting. No competing methodologies. EOS has to be your only focus."

"I understand that. And honestly, that's part of what appeals to me. I want to go all in on something that matters."

"Do you? Because I've seen people try to hedge. They keep their company, or they keep a side business, or they keep telling themselves they can always go back. Those people never make it. The ones who succeed are the ones who leap."

Alan thought about RTS. About Rachel and Kevin and the team he'd built. About the twenty-one years of his life poured into that company.

"I'll sit with it," he said.

"Good. We'll talk soon."

The line went quiet. Alan set his phone down and leaned back in his chair. Through the window, late-afternoon light slanted across the neighbor's yard, where their kids were playing in the freshly-fallen snow. Normal life, carrying on. He was about to step into something completely different.

He looked at the notes he'd written.

Passion. Purity. Story. Network. Emotional Intelligence.

Five ingredients. Five tests. And a community that would decide if he belonged.

He circled *Purity* again. Lauren was right. That was the one that scared him most.

For twenty-one years, his ideas had been the company. His instincts, his decisions, his way of doing things. RTS existed because of Alan Roth's vision. And now he was being asked to set all of that aside, to trust a system he didn't create, and to follow rather than lead.

Could he do that? Could he really subordinate his own ideas to someone else's methodology?

He thought about his experience as an EOS client. The system had worked. There was no denying that. EOS had transformed RTS from a chaotic mess into a thriving company. But along the way, he'd also used other tools he liked. Books on leadership. Frameworks from other consultants. Ideas he'd picked up at conferences and peer groups. Some of them had helped. Some hadn't. But they'd all been his to choose.

As an Implementer, he wouldn't have that flexibility. It would be EOS. Only EOS. Always EOS.

He thought about Sue in the session room. The way she never deviated from the process. The way she trusted the tools even when the team pushed back. The way the results spoke for themselves.

Maybe that was the point. Maybe Purity wasn't about giving up who you were. Maybe it was about recognizing that something bigger than yourself could be more powerful than your own ideas.

He'd have to sit with that.

Sarah knocked on the door an hour later. "How did it go?"

"Intense," Alan said. "Good intense. But intense."

"What did they ask?"

"Everything. Why I want to do this. Whether I have what it takes. Whether I'm willing to do it their way instead of my own." He looked at his notes. "They have these five ingredients they look for. And the community has to approve you before you can join."

"The community?"

"Other Implementers. They meet you at something called Boot Camp and decide if you belong." He shook his head. "It's not like any job application I've ever seen. It's more like... being invited into a family. And the family gets to vote on whether they want you."

Sarah sat down across from him. "And? Do you still want in?"

Alan looked at the legal pad. At the word *Purity* circled twice. At the question that he'd have to answer before he could move forward.

"More than ever," he said.

7

The Leap

"Real security doesn't come from having multiple options. It comes from being so good at one thing that you never have to worry about demand."

THE COMMUNITY ASSESSMENT happened three weeks after his call with Lauren.

Alan met with three Implementers over two days. Coffee meetings, video calls, and a lunch that lasted three hours. Lauren had explained that these conversations were about fit. Did Alan align with the community's Core Values? Did he get it, want it, and have the capacity to do this work? The Implementers who would assess him had done hundreds of these conversations. They knew what to look for.

The first Implementer, a man named Frank who'd been in the community for six years, focused on Core Values alignment.

"We have five Core Values in this community," Frank said. "Be Humbly Confident. Grow or Die. Help First. Do the Right Thing. Do What You Say. I'm going to ask you some questions to see if you're wired for these."

He started with Be Humbly Confident. "Tell me about a time you failed. Not a small failure. A real one. Something that kept you up at night."

Alan told him about a product launch in year eight of RTS. A new service offering that he'd been convinced would double their revenue. He'd invested heavily, hired a team, and marketed aggressively. It flopped. They lost three hundred thousand dollars and had to lay off four people.

"What did you learn?" Frank asked.

"That I'm not always right. That conviction isn't the same as correctness. That I need to test assumptions before betting the company on them."

Frank nodded. "Good. Some people can't admit failure. They spin everything into a success story. Those people don't make it in this work. Humbly Confident means thinking of yourself less, not thinking less of yourself. You have to be humble enough to know you don't have all the answers."

He moved through the other values. Do the Right Thing: "Tell me about a time you entered the danger, said the hard thing even though it was uncomfortable." Alan told him about Tom, the eight-year employee who was below the bar. Help First: "When have you given value without expecting anything in return?" Alan described mentoring young entrepreneurs through the Roundtable, spending hours helping them avoid his mistakes.

By the end, Frank seemed satisfied. "You're wired for these values, Alan. That matters more than anything else. Skills can be taught. Values can't."

The second Implementer, Jennifer, who'd been implementing for eight years, focused on GWC.

"You know what GWC means," she said. "Gets it, Wants it, Capacity to do it. That's how we evaluate whether someone belongs in a seat. Today, I'm evaluating whether you belong in the Implementer seat."

She started with Gets it. "What do you think this work actually is? Not what Lauren told you. What do you believe in your gut?"

Alan thought carefully. "It's not consulting. Consultants give answers. Implementers teach a system and hold people accountable for using it. The answer is always in the room. My job would be to help teams find their own answers, not give them mine."

Jennifer nodded. "Good. A lot of candidates think this is consulting with a different name. They wash out fast." She moved to Wants it. "Why do you want this? And I mean really want it. Not the polished answer. The real one."

"Because I watched Sue do it for six years, and I couldn't stop thinking about it. Because when I imagine the next twenty years of my life, this is the only thing that excites me. Because I've been where these entrepreneurs are, and I know how lost they feel, and I know there's a way out."

"That's wanting it." Jennifer leaned back in her chair. "Can I tell you something? I've been part of many business communities. Masterminds. Peer groups. Industry associations. None of them come close to what we have here."

"Everyone keeps saying that."

"Because it's true. The abundance mindset isn't just words on a wall. It's how people actually behave. When I was struggling in my first year, other Implementers sent me referrals. Not because they'd get anything in return. Just because they wanted me to succeed." Jennifer paused. "You'll see it for yourself at your first QCE. That abundance mindset creates a room full of people who should be competitors, but instead they are busy sharing their best secrets and cheering for your success as loudly as their own. It's unlike anything else in business."

Alan wanted to believe her. But he'd heard similar claims before from organizations that didn't live up to them.

"I know you're skeptical," Jennifer said, as if reading his mind. "That's okay. Healthy, even. But I promise you: when you experience it, you'll understand."

The third meeting was a video call with an Implementer in California named Rebecca. She focused on Capacity.

"Capacity isn't just about skills," Rebecca explained. "It's about your life. Your circumstances. Whether you have the bandwidth to do this work well."

She asked about his marriage, his family, and his support system. "This work can be lonely. You're not part of a company anymore. You don't have colleagues in the traditional sense. Your clients aren't your friends. You need people in your life who ground you, who remind you who you are when the work gets hard."

Alan told her about Sarah. Twenty-eight years of marriage. The way she'd supported him through the ups and downs of RTS. The way she'd noticed his passion for this before he'd fully admitted it to himself.

"She sounds like a good partner," Rebecca said. "You'll need her."

She also asked about his financial runway, his health, and his energy levels. "This work requires presence. Full engagement. If you're distracted by money problems, health issues, or family crises, you can't show up the way your clients need you to. Capacity means having the bandwidth to be fully present."

By the end of the call, Alan felt he'd been evaluated more thoroughly than in any job interview he'd ever had. These Implementers weren't just checking boxes. They were genuinely trying to determine if he belonged.

A week later, Lauren called with the news: he'd been approved.

"The community wants you," she said. "Boot Camp is in May. But before we finalize, I need to ask you something important. Do you have at least one year of living expenses set aside?"

"More than that," Alan said. "The sale closed a few months ago. I'm in good shape."

"Good. This is non-negotiable. You can't start this work from a place of financial desperation. Needy Implementers make bad decisions. They take on clients they shouldn't. They discount their fees. They compromise on Purity because they need the revenue. You need a financial runway. You have to be able to say no to the wrong opportunities because you're not desperate for the money."

"I understand."

"The first year is the hardest. You're building from scratch. Some months, you won't have any sessions. If you're worried about paying your mortgage, you can't show up fully present for your clients. So make sure you're financially prepared before you take this leap."

Alan said yes before he could talk himself out of it.

But saying yes to Boot Camp was the easy part. The hard part was what came next.

Not selling RTS. That was already done. The hard part was letting go of the identity he'd built over two decades.

For twenty-one years, he'd been Alan Roth, founder of RTS. That title had defined him, given him purpose, told him who he was in the world. He'd worn it like armor. When he walked into a room, people knew who he was. They knew what he'd built. They respected him for it.

Now he was nobody. Just a fifty-two-year-old guy with money in the bank and time on his hands. The business card in his wallet still said "RTS" because he hadn't gotten around to throwing it away. Every time he saw it, he felt a small pang of loss.

"You're grieving," Sarah said one night when she found him staring at the card. "That's normal. You gave twenty-one years of your life to that company. You can't just turn that off."

"I know. It's just..." He struggled to find the words. "I thought I'd feel free. I thought selling would be liberating. Instead, I feel like I'm floating, like I don't know who I am anymore."

"You're Alan Roth," Sarah said simply. "Husband. Father. Friend. Those things never changed. You just added 'founder' on top of them for a while. Now you're going to add something else: EOS Implementer."

"EOS Implementer." He smiled. "Has a nice ring to it."

* * *

He called Sue the week before Boot Camp.

"I'm having second thoughts," Alan admitted.

"About what specifically?"

"Everything. Whether I can do this. Whether I'm too old to start over. Whether anyone will actually hire me." He laughed bitterly. "I ran a company for twenty-one years. I thought I'd have more confidence than this."

"Confidence in running your company doesn't transfer to confidence in this work," Sue said. "They're different skills. Different muscles. You're a beginner again. That's uncomfortable for someone who's been an expert for two decades."

"So how do I get past it?"

"You don't get past it. You go through it. The fear, the doubt, the uncertainty, it's all part of the process. Every Implementer I know went through the same thing. The ones who made it were the ones who kept going anyway."

Alan was quiet for a moment. "What if I need to supplement my income with other services? Consulting, coaching, something to fill the gaps while I build my practice?"

Sue's voice turned serious. "Let me tell you about something I've seen in the community. There are Implementers who add products and services to their business. Consulting engagements. Coaching programs. Other frameworks bolted onto EOS. They tell themselves it's Help First. They say they're serving their clients better by offering more."

"That sounds reasonable."

"It sounds reasonable, but it's scarcity at work. They're hedging their bets. And here's what happens: their EOS practice never fully develops. They never get to twenty clients. They never experience the compounding effect of pure focus. Because every hour they spend on their side services is an hour they're not spending on building their EOS practice."

"So you're saying don't diversify."

"I'm saying trust the system. The Implementers who succeed are the ones who go all in. Pure EOS, nothing else. The ones who hedge, who keep their options open, they end up with mediocre results in multiple areas instead of extraordinary results in one."

Alan thought about that. It was the opposite of everything he'd learned in business. Diversification was supposed to reduce risk. Multiple revenue streams were supposed to provide security.

"It's counterintuitive," Sue said, as if reading his mind. "But the security doesn't come from having multiple options. It comes from being so good at one thing that you never have to worry about demand. Get to twenty clients delivering EOS purely, and you'll have more referrals than you can handle. That's real security. Not hedging."

"You're talking about burning the boats."

"I'm talking about burning the boats," Sue agreed. "You sold RTS. That was the first boat. But there are other boats you're still holding onto. The idea that you might go back to consulting. The backup plan you haven't admitted to yourself. The part of you that's keeping one foot on shore, just in case."

Alan felt exposed. He had been keeping a backup plan in the back of his mind. A half-formed idea that if the Implementer thing didn't work out, he could always start consulting. His network was strong. Companies would pay for his expertise.

"I can hear you thinking," Sue said. "Whatever backup plan you're holding onto, let it go. You can't do this halfway.

You can't keep one foot in your old life and one foot in this new one. The people who try to hedge, who keep their options open, who tell themselves they can always go back, they never make it. The ones who succeed are the ones who commit completely," she emphasized again.

"That's terrifying."

"Yes," Sue agreed. "It is. But here's what I've learned: the fear never goes away. You don't wait until you're not scared anymore. You act despite the fear. You burn the boats and trust that you'll find a way to win."

"What if I can't find clients? What if nobody wants to hire me?"

Sue laughed softly. "Alan, there are tens of thousands of companies in your backyard that need this. More than all the Implementers in the world could ever serve. The opportunity isn't scarce. It's abundant. The only question is whether you're willing to do the work."

"I've never had to sell myself before. RTS grew on referrals and reputation. I don't know how to start from zero."

"You won't be starting from zero. You have a network. You have relationships. You have a story that will resonate with every frustrated entrepreneur you meet. And you'll have the community behind you, teaching you, supporting you, holding you accountable." Sue paused. "The scarcity you're feeling right now? It's not real. It's just fear wearing a clever disguise."

* * *

The night before he left for Boot Camp, Alan sat on the back porch with Sarah.

"You know what I realized today?" he said. "When I started RTS, I was terrified. I had no idea what I was doing. No safety net. No guarantee of success. And it turned out to be the best thing I ever did."

"And now you're doing it again."

"And now I'm doing it again." He took her hand. "Maybe that's what life is. A series of leaps. Each one scarier than the last, but each one taking you somewhere you couldn't have imagined."

"That's very philosophical for a Sunday night."

Alan laughed. "I've had a lot of time to think."

Sarah was quiet for a moment. When she spoke, her voice was careful. "Can I ask you something? And I need you to really hear it, not just reassure me."

"Of course."

"What if you're wrong about this?" She turned to face him. "Not about the money. We're fine. But what if you get out there and discover you're not cut out for it? What if this doesn't fill the hole?" She paused, choosing her words. "I watched you pour yourself into RTS for twenty-one years. I watched what it cost you. The sleepless nights. The weight you carried. And now you've finally set that down, and instead of resting, you're picking up something new."

"Sarah..."

"I'm not finished." Her voice was gentle but firm. "I need to know: Are you running toward this, or are you running away from not knowing who you are without a company to build? Because if this doesn't work, Alan... if you bet your whole identity on becoming this thing and it falls apart..." She didn't finish the sentence.

The words hung between them. Alan felt the weight of them, the years of partnership that gave her the right to say them.

"I don't know," he said slowly. "I can't promise this will work. I can't even promise I'm doing it for the right reasons." He met her eyes. "But I know that when I imagine the next twenty years, this is the only thing that makes me feel alive. And I know that whatever happens, I'm not doing it alone this time. I have you. I have the community. I'm not carrying it by myself."

Sarah studied his face for a long moment. Then something in her softened.

"Okay," she said quietly. "Okay."

They sat in comfortable silence, watching the stars emerge. Tomorrow, he would fly to Detroit for Boot Camp. By the weekend, he would return as a Professional EOS Implementer. Official. Ready to help entrepreneurs transform their businesses the way Sue had transformed his.

Or at least, ready to try.

"You're going to be great at this," Sarah said quietly.

"How do you know?"

"Because you care. Because you've been where they are. Because you know what it feels like to be lost, and you know how to find the way out." She squeezed his hand. "And because you're Alan Roth. You've never failed at anything you truly committed to."

"First time for everything."

"Not this time," she said. "Not this time."

* * *

He had reading to do, preparation to complete, and a whole new career to learn. The path ahead was uncertain, terrifying, alive with possibility.

He was fifty-two years old, starting over, with no guarantee of success.

And for the first time in months, he felt completely ready.

The boats were burned. There was no going back. And somewhere out there, companies were waiting for him to help them find what he had found.

Tomorrow, the real work would begin.

8

Boot Camp

---

*"You can steal the fixtures, but you can't steal
the plumbing."*

ALAN'S FLIGHT TOUCHED down at Detroit Metro on a
bright May afternoon. He followed the signs toward baggage
claim, then realized he didn't need to go outside at all. The
Westin was attached directly to the airport, a glass-walled
corridor connecting the terminal to the hotel lobby. He'd heard
about this from Sue. You could fly in for Boot Camp and never
step outside until you flew home four days later. Opening
cocktail hour, two days of intensive training, the pre-QCE
reception, then QCE itself. The entire transformation happened
in one building.

His rolling bag clicked against the polished floor as he
walked. His mouth was dry. His palms were damp. Twenty-one
years of running a company, and here he was, nervous as a kid
on the first day of school.

He checked in, dropped his bag in his room, and spent an
hour reviewing his notes. The words blurred on the page. He
wasn't really reading. He was trying to quiet the voice that kept
asking whether he was ready for this.

At 5:45, he took the elevator down to the lobby. Through the windows, he could see planes taxiing in the fading light. He found Reflections, the bar tucked into the corner of the lobby, and spotted a cluster of people who had the same look he imagined he did: accomplished professionals trying to hide their nervousness behind confident postures.

The reception was being held in a nearby conference room. Alan got a drink first, letting the cold glass ground him. Then he walked in.

The space had been transformed into a casual gathering area. A handful of people were already there, the nervous energy of anticipation filling the air. Alan counted heads. Including himself, there were about a dozen aspiring Implementers milling about, sizing each other up with the careful assessment of experienced business leaders. He recognized the body language. These were people who'd spent careers reading rooms, building teams, and making decisions. And right now, every one of them looked slightly off-balance. It was comforting, somehow, to know he wasn't alone.

A woman in her mid-forties caught his eye and walked over. "Patricia Chen," she said, extending her hand.

Alan smiled as he shook it. "Alan Roth. I'm just getting settled in. My Implementer, Sue Hawkes, told me this was the best place to start the next chapter."

"Sue Hawkes? I know her well," Patricia said, her expression warming. "She's a legend in this community. It's a tight-knit group here—everyone seems to know everyone, or at least knows someone who knows someone. It's part of what drew me here in the first place."

A tall man in his early fifties joined them. "Robert Kim," he said, shaking hands with both. "Sold my logistics company about six months ago. Finally."

"Finally?" Alan asked.

Robert laughed, but there was weight behind it. "I made the decision to become an Implementer two years ago. Went through the whole assessment process, got approved, was ready to burn the boats." He shook his head. "Then my wife had some health issues. Had to put everything on hold to be there for her. Took longer than expected to sell the company, too. Buyers kept falling through. But I never stopped preparing. Read everything I could get my hands on. Practiced the 90-Minute Meeting on anyone who'd sit still long enough." He grinned. "My kids stopped visiting for a while there."

Alan laughed, but he understood. He'd done the same thing. Sarah had listened to him practice until she could probably deliver the VTH script herself.

"The waiting was hard," Robert continued. "Watching other people go through Boot Camp while I was stuck on the sidelines. But I'm here now. That's what matters."

A woman in her late forties stepped to the front of the room and raised her hand to get everyone's attention. "Good evening, everyone. I'm Maria Santos, your Boot Camp Teacher. Welcome to EOS Implementer Boot Camp."

She gestured to a man standing by the door. "This is David Chen, your Boot Camp Coach. I teach the content. David will be your ongoing resource as you build your practice. He's the one you'll call when you're stuck, when you have questions, or when you need someone who's been in your shoes."

David waved. "We'll get to know each other well over the next few months. My job is to make sure you don't feel alone out there."

The evening was informal by design. No agenda, just a chance to meet each other, share what they were excited about, and surface any concerns.

"What are you most excited about?" Maria asked the room. "And what concerns do you have coming in?"

One by one, they shared. Former CEOs. Entrepreneurs who'd built and sold companies. Executives who'd led hundreds of employees. Alan recognized the look in their eyes because he'd seen it in his own mirror for months. Fire. Purpose. A hunger for something more.

When it was his turn, Alan kept it simple. "I'm excited to finally be here. My concern? That I'll slip back into consultant mode and try to solve everyone's problems instead of helping them find their own answers."

Maria nodded. "That's a good concern to have. We'll be addressing that head-on tomorrow."

* * *

Tuesday morning arrived fast. Breakfast at 6:30, then into the training room by 7:45. The setup was simple. Whiteboards lined three walls. Chairs were arranged in a horseshoe, each with a thick Boot Camp Manual on the seat. Alan picked his up and felt the weight of it, the three-ring binder stuffed with session guides, process checklists, and templates. Everything an Implementer needed to deliver EOS purely, all in one place. No conference table. No screens. No technology at all, really. Just whiteboards, markers, and people. It was the exact same Spartan setup Sue had used for six years. Alan felt a surge of comfort in the familiarity; he knew from experience that in a room like this, there was nowhere for the truth to hide.

At precisely 8:00 a.m., Maria stepped to the front of the room.

"Let me be clear about what's happening here," Maria began. As she spoke, Alan instinctively reached for his pocket to ensure his phone was silenced and tucked away, a habit Sue had drummed into him years ago. He glanced around; most of the room was doing the same. "You've already been accepted into this community. The assessment you went through, the conversations with other Implementers, that was your vetting. You wouldn't be sitting in these chairs if you hadn't been approved. So this isn't about whether you belong. You do."

Alan felt something loosen in his chest. He hadn't realized how much residual anxiety he'd been carrying.

"These next two days are about two things," Maria continued, writing on the whiteboard. "First, understanding. When all the dust settles, you'll clearly understand the journey you're embarking on. The history, philosophy, and psychology behind EOS. What it takes to deliver a great 90-Minute Meeting. What you need to be ready for when you conduct your first Focus Day. How to build and live The EOS Life as an Implementer."

She wrote "JOIN FORCES" on the board.

"Second, we want to confirm you're excited and ready to join forces with us on this journey. By Thursday, you'll have experienced your first Quarterly Collaborative Exchange, or QCE, and be ready to hit the ground running."

The morning moved fast. Check-in first, where each Boot Camper shared their story, their "why," and their expectations. Alan listened carefully as his fellow trainees revealed their journeys. The patterns were familiar. Frustration with the limitations of their previous roles. The desire to make a bigger impact. The pull toward helping other entrepreneurs avoid the struggles they'd experienced.

Then came the EOS Story. Maria walked them through the history: Gino Wickman's early experiments in 2000, the decision to leverage rather than keep it to himself, Don Tinney proving the system could be replicated, and the abundance-minded business model that had transformed the community in 2009.

"The business was floundering," Maria explained. "Too few Implementers were gaining Traction. Gino and Don put a stake in the ground. Fix it or pull the plug. They completely reinvented the approach."

She continued through the franchise transition in 2021. "Here's what makes us different from any franchise you've ever heard of. No territories. No percentage of your revenue goes to EOS Worldwide. You pay a flat franchise fee, and everything you earn from your clients is yours. We succeed when you succeed. That's the abundance mindset in action."

Alan scribbled notes furiously. This was the context Sue had given him glimpses of, but hearing it laid out completely was different. He could see the through-line now.

* * *

After lunch, the focus shifted to what an Implementer actually does.

"You're going to hear three words over and over in this community," Maria said, writing on the whiteboard. "Teach. Coach. Facilitate."

She circled each word.

"Teaching is giving them the tools and concepts. The Accountability Chart. The V/TO. The Meeting Pulse. You're transferring knowledge they don't have yet."

She pointed to the second word. "Coaching is holding them accountable. It's having the hard conversations. It's calling them out when they're not doing what they said they'd do. It's caring enough about their success that you're willing to make them uncomfortable." She paused. "A lot of Implementers are comfortable with teaching. Fewer are comfortable with coaching. But the coaching is where the real breakthroughs happen."

She pointed to the third word. "Facilitating is helping them discover their own answers. The answer is always in the room. Your job is to draw it out, not to provide it. If you give them answers, they won't own them. If they discover the answers themselves, they'll fight for them."

Maria looked around the room. "All three matter. You can't be a great Implementer if you're only good at one or two. Master all three."

Alan thought about Sue. How she'd taught them the tools. How she'd coached Alan through letting go of RTS. How she'd facilitated sessions where the team found their own solutions. All three. Always all three.

Maria paused and looked around the room.

"Before we go any further, I need to talk about something that will determine whether you succeed or fail as an Implementer. EOS purity."

She walked to the whiteboard and wrote the word in capital letters.

"The world wants and expects EOS. The books, the videos, the conferences, the thousands of companies already running on EOS—they've made it clear what pure EOS looks and feels like. That's what clients want. If you deliver your own version, they'll either not hire you or not get the same results."

She turned back to face them. "Purity means following the EOS Proven Process. Teaching the EOS tools as laid out in the guides. Not adding your own twist. Not borrowing pieces from other methodologies. Not skipping steps because you think you know better."

Alan felt that familiar twinge of resistance. He had already prepared for this during his vetting call with Lauren. He knew that his twenty-one years of business experience would make following a script his biggest hurdle, but staring at the reality of it still felt like a physical weight. He remembered Lauren's warning that his ego would be the first thing he would have to let go of. He knew it was the right move for the client, but that did not make suppressing his own "better" ideas any easier.

Maria must have seen something in his face. "I know what some of you are thinking. You've built companies. You've solved hard problems. You have valuable experience. Why should you suppress all that and just deliver someone else's system?"

She let the question hang.

"Here's why. Picture all of our clients in one room. Hundreds of companies. They all speak the same language. They all have the same experience. When one leadership team talks to another, they understand each other immediately. That only happens if every Implementer delivers the same system the same way."

She walked closer to the group. "And here's the other reason. The EOS tools have been tested on tens of thousands of companies. They work. Every time you deviate—every time you add your own idea or skip a step or try to improve the process—you're running an experiment on your client. And your experiment hasn't been tested on tens of thousands of companies. EOS has."

Alan thought about what Lauren had said during the vetting process. *Purity is what protects the client.*

"None of us is one hundred percent pure," Maria continued. "It's a journey. But the standard is a nine-plus purity rating. That means following the guides, doing your homework, questioning and challenging anything you don't understand, but doing it through the proper channels. Monday Calls. QCEs. Your coach. Not by freelancing in front of clients."

She paused again to let her words sink in before continuing. "If you don't want to be pure EOS, you can't be here. That's not a threat. It's just the reality. This community exists to deliver EOS to the world. If that's not what you want to do, there are plenty of other ways to help entrepreneurs."

Alan wrote in his notebook: *Purity = protecting the client. Trust the system.*

* * *

The afternoon shifted to the 90-Minute Meeting.

"This is where most of you will spend the next several months," Maria said. "Mastering this. The 90-Minute Meeting is not a sales pitch. It is a session. You must do it every time with a Warm Lead, and you must do it to the letter. There is so much psychology and sales built into this meeting. They must see the context. They must understand what they're about to get themselves into."

She walked them through each step. The Safe Island opening. The power of story. The About You section. The Tools. The Process. The close that wasn't really a close.

"At the end, you just ask, 'Any questions? Are you calling me, or am I calling you?'" Maria demonstrated. "That's it. No hard close. No pressure. You've given them tremendous value. Now you let them decide."

By mid-afternoon, they were practicing their stories in breakout sessions, getting feedback from David.

"Your story needs three punches," David explained. "Three data points that establish your credibility with decision makers. Remember who you're talking to: entrepreneurs running companies with ten to two hundred fifty employees. They need to know you've been where they are. You've walked the path. You're not some consultant who's only read about it in books."

He pointed to the whiteboard where Maria had written:

Punch 1: Built/ran a company (size, scope, credibility)

Punch 2: Hit the ceiling, implemented EOS (transformation)

Punch 3: Where you are now (why you're doing this)

"Sixty seconds. Three punches. That's your story."
When Alan's turn came, he stood and faced the group.

"I built a staffing company called RTS from scratch. Twenty-one years. Grew it to fifty employees and twelve million in revenue." He paused. "But for three of those years, we were stuck at eight million. I was working seventy hours a week, lying awake at night, and cycling through consultants who couldn't help. Then I implemented EOS with an Implementer named Sue Hawkes. In eighteen months, we broke through the ceiling and grew to twelve million with better margins and a leadership team that actually functioned. I got my life back." Another pause. "I sold RTS last year because I realized I wanted to spend the next chapter of my life helping other entrepreneurs experience what I experienced. That's why I'm here."

The room was quiet for a moment.

"That's a story," David said. "Decision makers will hear themselves in that. Three punches: you built something real, you hit the ceiling and broke through, and now you're here to help them do the same. Clean. Credible. Compelling."

Alan sat down, feeling something click into place. His story wasn't just backstory. It was his qualification. Every frustrated entrepreneur he'd meet would recognize pieces of themselves in those three punches.

* * *

The formal portion of Day 1 ended at 5:00 p.m., but the learning was far from over. After a quick dinner at 5:30, the group migrated back to the training room at 6:30. This evening session was different. The Boot Camp teacher was gone, leaving the room to the students for two hours of relaxed and peer-led 90-Minute Meeting practice. Without a coach watching their every move, the tension in the room finally began to thaw.

"This is where you build the muscle," Maria told them before releasing them for dinner. "You'll deliver the 90 as a tag team tomorrow morning. Tonight is your dress rehearsal."

The practice session was grueling. Alan stumbled through the Tools section, losing his place twice. Robert forgot the fee presentation entirely. Patricia nailed her story but rushed through the Process so fast that no one could follow.

"You're all going to be terrible tomorrow," the coach said cheerfully at 8:30. "And that's okay. This is the hardest 90-Minute Meeting you'll ever give. Get some rest. Tomorrow it gets real."

* * *

Wednesday morning, Day 2, started with the tag-team presentation. Each Boot Camper would take a section of the 90-Minute Meeting and deliver it to the group, with Maria and the coach playing the role of a skeptical leadership team.

"Here's how this works," Maria explained. "You'll go in order around the room. When I yell 'SWITCH,' whoever is presenting stops immediately, and the next person picks up exactly where they left off. No warning. No preparation. You have to know the material well enough to jump in at any moment."

Alan's stomach tightened. This was nothing like the structured practice from the night before.

Patricia started with the Safe Island opening, then moved into her story. She was halfway through when Maria's voice cut through the room.

"SWITCH!"

Robert jumped up and continued seamlessly into the About You section. He was explaining the purpose when Maria called out again.

"SWITCH!"

The next Boot Camper stumbled, recovered, and pressed on. They skipped the part where clients rate themselves on each of the Six Key Components. That would come in practice later. For now, it was about flow, about knowing where you were in the meeting at any moment.

When Alan's turn came, he was midway through The Tools section, drawing the EOS Model on the whiteboard. He'd just finished explaining the Six Key Components when his mind went completely blank. He stared at the whiteboard, marker frozen in mid-air.

"And the next tool is..." He drew a circle. Then another circle. Then, inexplicably, a triangle. "The... Accountability... Pyramid?"

The room erupted in laughter. There was no Accountability Pyramid in EOS.

"I have no idea where that came from," Alan admitted, his face reddening. "I think I just invented a new tool."

"Write that down," Robert called out. "We'll pitch it to Gino."

Maria was laughing too. "This is exactly why we do this exercise. Better to invent imaginary tools here than in front of a real client. Keep going."

Alan took a breath, found his place, and continued. The laughter had broken something loose in the room. They were all going to stumble. They were all going to look foolish at some point. And that was okay.

He'd just finished explaining The Accountability Chart when Maria yelled.

"SWITCH!"

He stopped mid-sentence. The next person jumped in without missing a beat, picking up exactly where Alan had stopped. It was disorienting and exhilarating at the same time.

By the time they finished the complete 90-Minute Meeting as a group, something had shifted. They weren't twelve individuals anymore. They were a team that had been through something together.

During the break, Alan found himself standing next to Patricia near the coffee station.

"Nervous about tomorrow?" she asked.

"A little. I'm not entirely sure what to expect from the QCE."

Patricia smiled. "I haven't lived it yet, but it's what an Implementer, Jennifer, described during my community assessment call. She told me to imagine a hundred Implementers from all over the country, all gathering to learn from each other and share best practices. No competition. No hidden agendas. Just people who genuinely want to help each other succeed."

"That sounds too good to be true."

"I know. I thought the same thing," Patricia paused. "I was skeptical, but Jennifer said I'd understand once I experienced it for myself."

"And do you? Understand, I mean?"

Patricia laughed. "Ask me again tomorrow night. But from what I've seen so far, I'm starting to believe her."

* * *

The rest of Day 2 was dedicated to business development. David took over for this section.

"Three hours," he said, "designed to teach you how to generate Warm Leads, convert them to 90-Minute Meetings, and conduct one Focus Day every single month."

He walked to the whiteboard and wrote: 4-2-1.

"This is your formula. This is your mantra. Four Warm Leads every month, which will lead to two 90-Minute Meetings, which will lead to one new client conducting a Focus Day. That's the math. That's what we want you laser-focused on."

He paused and picked up a book from the table.

"Here's something important to understand. The ninety-day cycle isn't an EOS invention. It's based on the science of human focus. Research shows that humans can only maintain intense focus on a goal for about ninety days before fatigue sets in, distractions multiply, and priorities start to blur."

He held up the book. "If you haven't read *Essentialism* by Greg McKeown, put it on your list. Many Implementers consider it essential reading. The core idea is simple: we can do anything, but we can't do everything. The ninety-day Rocks cycle forces that discipline. It forces leadership teams to say no to the merely good so they can say yes to the truly great."

Alan thought about the years at RTS when everything had felt urgent. When every priority competed with every other priority. When he'd tried to do everything and ended up doing nothing particularly well.

"The same principle applies to building your practice," the coach continued. "The 4-2-1 system works because it forces focus. You're not trying to do a hundred things. You're doing the few things that actually move the needle. Focus compounds. Distraction dissipates. Remember that."

Alan studied the numbers. It seemed almost too simple. Four leads. Two meetings. One client. Every month.

"Let me unpack this," the coach continued. "A Warm Lead is a decision-maker of a business willing to talk with you about EOS. If it's not a decision-maker, it's not a Warm Lead. If they're not willing to talk with you about EOS, it's not a Warm Lead."

He pulled out the BizDev Checklist and walked them through it section by section. The 7-Day Launch. The Weekly Checklist. The Monthly activities. The yearly touchpoints.

"In your first seven days after Boot Camp, you'll identify your Warm Leads, identify your connectors, build your email list, familiarize yourself with the branding guidelines, perfect your one-minute story, master the Warm Call, set up your EOS email and microsite, update your LinkedIn profile, send an announcement to your network, mail 100 copies of *Traction*, order Leadership Team Manuals, practice the 90-Minute Meeting daily, and set your session fee."

Alan looked at the list. It was overwhelming. And also strangely reassuring. There was a system for this, too.

"Every week," the coach continued, "you'll do one to three activities to generate a new Warm Lead. You'll do a Warm Call with that lead. You'll update your connectors. You'll mail *Traction* to book process leads. You'll obsess about your list. You'll practice the 90-Minute Meeting. And you'll participate in the Monday Calls."

Robert raised his hand. "Does this actually work? I mean, the math seems almost too clean. Four leads, two meetings, one client. What's the catch?"

The coach smiled. "The catch is you have to actually do it. Every week. Without fail. Don Sasse did ten Focus Days in his first quarter. When we asked him what he did, he said, 'I just followed the script you gave me.' That's it. Follow the process. Do the work. The results come."

Alan wanted to believe it. But part of him was skeptical. He'd built a company from nothing. He knew that business development was never this linear. There were always variables, unexpected obstacles, and deals that fell through at the last minute.

"I can see the skepticism on some of your faces," the coach said, as if reading his mind. "Good. Be skeptical. But also trust the process. This checklist was built on years of watching some people succeed and many others fail. It's not theory. It's lever-pulling. Everything on this list comes from studying what works and what doesn't work."

He paused and looked around the room, her expression turning serious.

"I need to be very clear about something. Building your practice is 100 percent up to you. Not EOS Worldwide. Not your coach. Not your T-Group. You." He let that sink in. "From time to time, EOS Worldwide may send you a Warm Lead. Someone fills out a form on the website, requests an Implementer in your area, and we pass it along. But these are gifts, not guarantees. You cannot build a business waiting for leads to show up in your inbox. The Implementers who fail are the ones who think someone else is going to build their pipeline for them. The Implementers who succeed are the ones who take complete ownership of their business development from day one."

Patricia raised her hand. "So how many leads should we expect from EOS Worldwide?"

"Expect zero," the coach said flatly. "Any lead you receive is a bonus. A pleasant surprise. But your plan should assume you're generating every single Warm Lead yourself. That's why the 4-2-1 system exists. That's why The List exists. That's why the connector process exists. These are your tools. Your responsibility. Your business."

Alan appreciated the directness. No false promises. No inflated expectations. Just the truth about what it would take.

He had them fill in their own weekly activities. The three things they would commit to doing every week to generate Warm Leads. Alan wrote: Call five people in my network. Meet with two connectors. Mail *Traction* to ten potential leads.

"If you fly home Thursday night," the coach said, "I want you on your laptop on the flight, updating your LinkedIn profile, reaching out to Warm Leads. Friday morning, you're running full blast. Saturday, Sunday, Monday. Every single day. This is how you build a practice."

* * *

After the Biz Dev section, they covered Implementer Operations. The pathway from Professional to Certified to Expert. The standards they'd need to meet. The community resources available to them.

Then they built their own V/TOs. Alan sat with his manual, answering the eight questions for his own Implementer practice. His 10-Year Target. His 3-Year Picture. His one-year plan. His Rocks for the first ninety days.

"This isn't optional," the coach said as they worked. "You run your practice on EOS, just like you'll teach your clients to run their companies. If you don't eat your own cooking, they'll smell it."

Next came the Scorecard. Alan filled in the weekly measurables he'd track: new Warm Leads, total prospects in his pipeline, 90-Minute Meetings scheduled, Focus Days delivered, average client rating, days billed, and revenue collected. Every week, he'd update these numbers. Every Monday Call, he might be asked to share them with the community.

Finally, they received The List. A spreadsheet template with tabs for tracking everything: companies by stage, connectors by year, conversion rates, stats, and revenue predictions. This would become the nerve center of his business development.

"Implementers who succeed obsess over The List," the coach said. "They update it religiously. They know their numbers. They can tell you exactly where every prospect is in the pipeline and which connectors are generating leads. The ones who fail? They treat it like homework they can skip."

It was real now. Not a dream. Not a plan. A business he was building.

* * *

That evening, the Boot Camp trainees joined the QCE Welcome Reception at 6:00 p.m. Alan walked into the hotel ballroom and stopped short.

The room was filled with Implementers. Not just the twelve people from his Boot Camp class, but dozens more. Maybe a hundred. They were arriving from all over the country for tomorrow's Quarterly Collaborative Exchange, and tonight was the kickoff.

The energy was palpable. Clusters of people reconnecting like old friends. Laughter echoing off the walls. Name tags everywhere, some with "NEW EOS IMPLEMENTER" badges like Alan's, others with years of certification noted.

"This is the community," Robert said, appearing at Alan's elbow with two drinks. "Everyone Maria was talking about. They all come together every quarter."

Alan took the offered glass and scanned the room. These were people who had been where he was standing. People who had made the leap, built their practices, and transformed companies. Some looked like seasoned executives. Others looked like they could be his neighbors. All of them had chosen this path.

A woman in her fifties approached them with a warm smile. "First QCE?"

"That obvious?" Alan gestured at his badge.

"The badge helps, but it's mostly the expression. Like a kid on the first day of school." She extended her hand. "I'm Diane. Eight years in. Best decision I ever made."

Over the next hour, Alan met more Implementers than he could count. Each one asked about his background, his market, his "why." Each one offered advice, encouragement, or a connection. Nobody competed for attention. Nobody tried to sell anything. They just... helped.

Patricia caught his eye across the room and smiled. She'd been right. Lauren had been right. There was nothing like this community.

"This is what 'Help First' looks like," Robert said as they finally found seats at a table for dinner. "It's not just a slogan."

Patricia joined them, along with two Certified Implementers from Texas who had offered to answer questions about building a practice. The conversation flowed easily, a mix of tactical advice and philosophical discussion about what it meant to do this work.

The taller of the two Texans set down his fork. "The first year is hard," he said. "But look around this room." He gestured at the crowded reception hall. "Every single person here wants you to succeed. That's not normal in business. That's what makes this community different."

Alan thought about his years running RTS. The isolation. The sense that he was figuring everything out alone. This was the opposite. A room full of people who understood the journey because they were living it too.

* * *

Thursday was QCE day.

Alan turned the badge over in his hands before clipping it on. White background, bold letters: "NEW EOS IMPLEMENTER." Such a simple thing. A piece of plastic with a clip on the back. But holding it, he felt the weight of everything that had led to this moment. The years at RTS. The ceiling he'd hit. The transformation he'd experienced. The leap he'd taken.

He thought about the entrepreneurs he would help. The leadership teams he would sit with. The businesses that would transform because he'd chosen this path.

He clipped the badge to his shirt.

This is who I am now.

He walked into the conference center at 8:00 a.m. The energy from last night's reception had carried over. The same hundred Implementers, now gathered for a full day of learning, sharing, and connecting.

The day was structured around breakout sessions on specific tools, practice exercises, and story swaps, in which experienced Implementers shared their hardest client situations and how they'd navigated them.

During lunch, Alan found himself at a table with three Certified Implementers, all of whom had been where he was standing just a few years ago.

"The first year is the hardest," one of them said. "You're learning the tools, building your confidence, trying to fill your calendar. But if you stick with it, if you stay pure and stay connected to this community, it works. The system works."

"What about T-Groups?" Alan asked. "How do those work?"

"You find your own," she said. "Three to five Implementers at similar stages who meet regularly for peer accountability. Nobody assigns you to one. You build those relationships yourself, usually with people you meet at QCEs or on the Monday Calls. People you click with. People who'll hold you accountable and call you out when you're off track."

Alan thought about Robert. Two years of waiting. Still showing up. Still preparing. That was the kind of person you wanted in your corner.

"What's your biggest piece of advice for someone just starting?" he asked.

"Trust the process," she said without hesitation. "When you're in front of a leadership team, and they're struggling, and every instinct in your body is screaming at you to just give them the answer, don't. Ask another question. Write what they say on the board. Let them discover it themselves. That's when the magic happens."

* * *

By the time the QCE concluded at 5:00 p.m., Alan was exhausted but energized. He found Robert in the lobby, both of them waiting for their shuttle to the terminal.

"We should stay in touch," Robert said. "Seriously. Weekly calls. Hold each other accountable. Maybe build toward a T-Group once we find the right people."

Alan nodded. "I was thinking the same thing."

"Deal." Robert extended his hand, and they shook. "You know what's funny? I spent thirty years building a logistics company. I thought that was hard. Moving freight across continents, managing drivers, dealing with customs nightmares. And it was hard. But this?" He gestured vaguely at the conference center behind them. "This is a different kind of hard."

"Because it's not about systems and processes," Alan said. "It's about people. It's about sitting in front of a leadership team that's stuck and frustrated and scared, and helping them find their own way through. You can't brute-force that. You can't out-work it. You can only be present. Really present."

"And trust the process."

"And trust the process."

A black sedan pulled up to the curb. Robert grabbed his bag.

"Same time Monday?" he asked. "After the Monday Morning Call?"

"I'll be there," Alan said.

He watched Robert's car pull away, then turned to look back at the conference center one more time. Four days ago, he'd walked through those doors for a happy hour reception, unsure what to expect. He was leaving as something different. Not an Implementer yet. Not really. But on the path. Learning to unlearn. Discovering how much he didn't know about helping others find what he'd been so quick to give away.

His phone buzzed. A text from Sarah.

How was it?

Alan thought for a long moment before typing his reply.

Hardest thing I've ever done. Can't wait to do more.

His rideshare arrived. Alan climbed in, pulled out his phone, and started updating his LinkedIn profile. Four Warm Leads. Two 90-Minute Meetings. One new client. Every month.

He still wasn't sure he believed it would be that simple. But he was willing to follow the script and find out.

The boats were burned. The training had begun. And somewhere out there, his first client was waiting.

9

The First Client

"The answer is always in the room."

THE FIRST SEVEN days after Boot Camp were a blur of activity.

Alan sat at the kitchen table with a hundred copies of *Traction* stacked in front of him, a box of padded envelopes, and a sheet of address labels. Two thousand dollars' worth of books. Sarah had raised an eyebrow when the boxes arrived, but she hadn't said anything.

He'd asked his connectors for names using the process they'd taught at Boot Camp. The email was simple: *I'd like to send a copy of* Traction *as a gift from you to people you think would benefit from it. If you give me names and addresses, I'll mail it with a note that says you thought they'd enjoy it.*

The responses surprised him. His former attorney sent five names. His accountant sent three. A friend from his Roundtable sent twelve. Within a week, he had more than enough names to fill out the hundred.

Now he sat with a stack of sticky notes, writing the same message over and over in his neatest handwriting: *Mike Henderson thought you'd enjoy and benefit from this copy of* Traction. Then the next one: *Bill Patterson thought you'd enjoy and benefit from this copy of* Traction. Each book got a sticky note on the cover, his business card tucked into the front pages, and a padded envelope with a printed label.

Sarah brought him coffee around 9 p.m. "How many left?"

"Thirty-two."

She picked up one of the completed envelopes. "This is a lot of faith in a book."

"It's not faith in the book. It's faith in the process." Alan stretched his back. "Every successful Implementer I talked to at QCE said the same thing. Mail the books. Don't follow up. Don't sell. Just give value and let it work."

"And if it doesn't work?"

"Then I mail more books."

By midnight, all one hundred envelopes were sealed and labeled. The next morning, he loaded them into his car and drove to the post office, where the clerk looked at the stack with something between amusement and respect.

"Starting a business?" she asked.

"Something like that."

* * *

The connector meetings were harder than the books.

The process was straightforward: Help first for fifty minutes. Ask for help in the last five. But Alan kept catching himself wanting to talk about EOS, wanting to pitch, wanting to shortcut the relationship-building because he was anxious for results.

His meeting with Mike Henderson was the one that finally clicked.

They met at a coffee shop in Edina on a Tuesday morning. Alan had known Mike for years through the Roundtable, but they'd never had a real conversation about Mike's business.

"What's working for you right now?" Alan asked after they'd caught up on families and mutual friends.

Mike laughed. "You want the honest answer or the polite one?"

"The honest one."

For the next forty-five minutes, Mike talked. His company was stuck. Revenue had plateaued. His leadership team wasn't aligned. He was working sixty hours a week and felt like he was running in place.

Alan listened. He asked questions. When Mike described a specific frustration with his operations manager, Alan walked him through IDS on a napkin. Identify the issue. Discuss it openly. Solve it with a clear action.

"That's good," Mike said, studying the napkin. "That's really good. Why haven't I thought of it that way before?"

"Because you're too close to it. Sometimes it takes an outside perspective."

By the end of the hour, Alan had given Mike three concrete ideas to try with his team. He hadn't mentioned EOS once. Hadn't asked for anything. Had just shown up and helped.

As they were packing up to leave, Mike said, "So tell me more about what you're doing now. This EOS thing."

Alan gave him the sixty-second version. His story with RTS. The transformation. His decision to become an Implementer.

"Would you feel comfortable introducing me to some of your friends?" Alan asked. "People who might be going through what you're going through?"

"Absolutely." Mike pulled out his phone. "Actually, there's a guy I've been meaning to connect you with. Steve Polanski. Runs a commercial HVAC company. Good guy, but he's been struggling. Reminds me of you, back before you figured things out."

"I'd appreciate the introduction."

"I'll text him right now. Tell him to expect your call."

That was the first Warm Lead Alan generated in Minneapolis. Not from a cold call. Not from a marketing campaign. From helping someone for fifty minutes and asking for five.

* * *

The night before his first Focus Day, Alan called David Chen.

"How are you feeling?" David asked.

"Terrified," Alan admitted. "I've practiced the 90-Minute Meeting a hundred times. I know the Focus Day agenda cold. But this is real. What if I freeze up?"

"You won't freeze up. You're more prepared than you think." David's voice was calm, reassuring. "Remember, you're not inventing anything tomorrow. You're delivering a proven process. Trust the guides. Follow the agenda. The tools work."

"What if the client pushes back? What if they challenge me?"

"Then you enter the danger. You don't have to have all the answers. The answer is always in the room. Your job is to facilitate, not to fix." David paused. "Alan, I've seen a lot of new Implementers come through Boot Camp. You have the story. You have the experience. Now you just need to trust yourself enough to deliver what you already know."

They talked for another twenty minutes. By the time Alan hung up, the trembling in his hands had quieted. Not gone. But manageable.

* * *

Three weeks after Boot Camp, Alan sat in his car outside a glass-fronted office building in the Minneapolis suburb of Eden Prairie, his hands trembling slightly on the steering wheel.

His backyard. Exactly where the system said to build.

The lead had come through Mike Henderson, just as the process promised it would. Alan had sent Steve a copy of *Traction* with a handwritten note. Steve called three days later. "I read the whole thing in one sitting," Steve had said. "It's like Wickman was describing my company. When can we talk?"

They'd scheduled the 90-Minute Meeting for the following week. Steve had brought his leadership team of four: his operations manager, sales director, CFO, and HR director. The meeting had gone well. Better than well. By the end, Steve was ready to commit.

"When can we start?" Steve had asked.

Now, three weeks later, Alan was sitting in the parking lot of Polanski Mechanical, about to facilitate his first Focus Day.

His phone buzzed. A text from Robert Kim.

First Focus Day today, right? You've got this. Trust the process.

Alan smiled. They'd been talking every week since Boot Camp, comparing notes, holding each other accountable. Robert had his first 90-Minute Meeting scheduled for the following Tuesday.

Thanks. Heading in now.

He grabbed his bag and checked the contents one more time. *Traction* book. V/TO for each leader. Business cards. Proven Process handouts. Focus Day Overview. Leadership Team Manual. Legal pad, pen, folder. Client profile sheet. Whiteboard markers in three colors. He'd ordered his own set after Boot Camp, unwilling to trust whatever might be available in a client's conference room.

The props were there. The question was whether he was.

He thought about the fee presentation he'd practiced hundreds of times. "Here's the way my fee works. I work on a daily fee. It's four thousand dollars per day, and it's fully guaranteed. What that means is, I'll ask you to bring a check to the session. At the end of the day, if you didn't get value, you won't pay me. It's that simple."

Four thousand dollars. The number still felt strange in his mouth. At RTS, he'd closed deals worth ten times that without breaking a sweat. But this was different. This was him. His value. His expertise. His ability to help.

He checked his reflection in the rearview mirror and walked toward the building.

* * *

Steve Polanski was exactly what Alan had expected. Mid-fifties, with the calloused hands of someone who'd started his career actually installing HVAC systems before building a company that now employed sixty people. His leadership team filed into the conference room with the wary skepticism of people who'd been through too many failed initiatives.

The room smelled like industrial cleaner and fresh coffee, the scent of a company trying to make a good impression.

"Thanks for making the time," Alan said as they settled into their seats. The whiteboard was adequate. Not great, but adequate.

"Mike speaks highly of you," Steve said. "Said you transformed your company with this stuff. So here we are."

Alan began with the Context section, explaining the day's objectives and giving them a glimpse of the journey ahead. Then he shared his story. RTS. The ceiling. The transformation. The sale.

"I've been where you are," he said, looking around the table. "I know what it feels like to work seventy hours a week and still feel like you're falling behind. I know the frustration of having a team that doesn't seem to get it. And I know there's a way out. That's what we're going to work on today."

The room shifted slightly. He had their attention.

The morning session focused on the Accountability Chart. Alan walked them through the three major functions, drawing the familiar structure on the whiteboard. Sales/Marketing. Operations. Finance/Admin.

"Before we put names in boxes," Alan said, "we need to get the structure right. So for the next few hours, I'm going to ask you to do something uncomfortable. I need you to figuratively fire everyone."

Steve's operations manager, a woman named Dana, looked uncomfortable. "Fire everyone?"

"Just for the next few hours," Alan said, forcing a slight smile. "We'll hire everyone back before lunch. The point is to separate structure from people. We need to get the structure right first. Then we'll figure out who belongs where."

The first two hours went smoothly. They identified the major functions. They debated the roles under each function. They built out the structure without naming names, just as Alan had practiced.

Then they started putting people in seats.

"I think Dana should be the Integrator," Steve said.

Dana's eyes widened. "You mean run the company? Day to day?"

"You already do half of it," Steve said. "You just don't have the authority or the accountability."

Alan watched Dana carefully. Something was wrong. Her body language had shifted. She was pulling back, crossing her arms.

"Dana," Alan said, "what's going on?"

"Nothing," Dana said quickly. Too quickly.

Alan felt the familiar urge rise up. Move on. Don't push. Keep the peace. This was his first client. If he pushed too hard and Dana shut down, the whole session could fall apart. Steve might not schedule Vision Building. Word might get back to Mike that Alan had been too aggressive.

But there was an elephant in the room. Everyone could feel it.

Enter the danger.

The phrase echoed in his mind. Maria's voice from Boot Camp. *"We take a risk and walk into the potential conflict. We are fanatical about resolution and comfortable with conflict. Go there when you see eye rolls. You don't always know the outcome or have the answer."*

Alan hesitated. Four thousand dollars was sitting in an envelope on the table. Was he really going to risk it on his first day?

Then another phrase surfaced, one of the Core Values: Do the Right Thing. And the line beneath it that he'd memorized during Boot Camp: *No amount of money is worth betraying a trust.*

If he let this go, he wouldn't be helping them. He'd be protecting himself. And that wasn't why he'd burned the boats. That wasn't why he'd walked away from RTS. That wasn't why he was sitting in a conference room in Eden Prairie, fifteen minutes from home, on a random Tuesday in October.

"Dana," Alan said again, his voice steadier now, "I can see something's bothering you. We're not going to be able to move forward until we address it. What's really going on?"

The room went silent. Steve shifted in his seat. The CFO looked down at the table.

Dana stared at Alan for a long moment. Then her shoulders dropped.

"I don't know if I want it," she said quietly. "The Integrator seat. I've been doing the work for years, but I never signed up to run the company. Steve is the one everyone looks to. I'm just..." She trailed off.

"Just what?" Alan asked.

"Just the person who keeps things from falling apart."

Steve leaned forward. "Dana, I had no idea you felt that way."

"Because you never asked," Dana said. There was no anger in her voice. Just exhaustion. "You assumed I wanted more responsibility. You assumed I was angling for a bigger role. But I'm not. I like operations. I like solving problems. I don't want to be in charge of everything."

The silence stretched. Alan let it sit, resisting the urge to fill it.

Finally, Steve spoke. "Then who?"

"That's what we need to figure out," Alan said. "But we couldn't figure it out until we knew what Dana really wanted. Now we can have an honest conversation."

The next hour was uncomfortable. They explored alternatives. They debated whether to hire someone from outside. They discussed what Dana actually wanted her role to be. It was messy and uncertain and nothing like the clean Accountability Chart exercise Alan had practiced in his basement.

But by the end, they had something real. Dana would stay in operations, with a clearly defined seat and clearly defined roles. Steve would begin the search for an Integrator, someone who actually wanted the job. And everyone in the room understood that the structure they were building wasn't just boxes on a whiteboard. It was a commitment to honesty.

* * *

The afternoon moved faster. Rocks. Meeting Pulse. Scorecard. Each tool built on the foundation they'd laid in the morning, a foundation that felt sturdier now because they'd been willing to enter the danger.

Midway through setting Rocks, something happened that Alan would remember for years.

Steve's sales director, a man named Tony who'd been quiet most of the day, was struggling to articulate his Rock for the quarter. He kept describing activities instead of outcomes. "Make more calls. Visit more clients. Work harder."

Alan didn't correct him. He just asked questions. "What would success look like at the end of ninety days? If you crushed this quarter, what would be different?"

Tony stared at the table. The room was silent. Alan let it sit.

Then Tony looked up. "We'd have three new accounts in the industrial sector. That's what's been missing. We keep chasing the same old clients instead of breaking into new verticals."

"So what's the Rock?"

"Three new industrial accounts closed by the end of the quarter."

Steve leaned forward. "Tony, we've been talking about industrial for two years. Why hasn't it happened?"

"Because I never made it a Rock," Tony said slowly, as if hearing himself for the first time. "It was always 'someday.' Something I'd get to after the urgent stuff. But if it's a Rock..." He paused. "Then it's the priority. Not the urgent stuff."

Alan watched the shift happen in real time. Tony's posture changed. His eyes sharpened. He wasn't just agreeing to a task. He was committing to an outcome that mattered.

This, Alan realized, was what he'd been searching for. Not the teaching. Not the tools. This moment. The moment when someone saw something they couldn't see before. The moment when possibility opened up because someone finally asked the right question.

He hadn't given Tony the answer. He'd just held the space until Tony found it himself.

The answer is always in the room.

For the first time since he'd walked into the building that morning, Alan wasn't nervous. He was exactly where he was supposed to be.

By 4:30, they were in the Conclude section. Alan asked each person to share his or her feedback and rate the day on a scale of one to ten.

The CFO went first. "I've been in leadership meetings for twenty years, and I've never seen a conversation like the one we had this morning. The honesty. The willingness to actually say what we're thinking. Ten."

Dana was next. "I walked in here this morning thinking I was about to be handed a job I didn't want. I'm leaving knowing that I have a seat that actually fits me. That's worth more than I can say. Nine."

The sales director gave it an eight, noting that he wished they'd had more time to dig into specific issues but acknowledging that the foundation was solid.

Steve went last.

"Twenty-three years," he said. "Twenty-three years of assuming I knew what my people wanted. Twenty-three years of putting people in roles without asking if they actually wanted to be there. That conversation with Dana this morning was the most important conversation I've had in this company in a decade." He paused. "And it almost didn't happen. You pushed, Alan. You could have let it go, but you didn't. That took guts. Ten."

Alan felt something shift in his chest. He'd entered the danger. He'd risked the check. And it had made all the difference.

* * *

As they were packing up, Steve approached him with the envelope.

"I assume you want this," Steve said, holding it out.

Alan took it. Four thousand dollars. His first session fee. Earned, not given.

"Same time next month for Vision Building?" Steve asked.

"I'll send the calendar invite tomorrow," Alan said.

They shook hands. Steve held on for an extra moment.

"Thank you," he said. "I mean it. This was exactly what we needed."

Alan walked to his car as the afternoon sun cast long shadows across the parking lot. He sat behind the wheel for a long moment, holding the envelope, letting it sink in.

He'd done it. Not perfectly. There were moments he'd talked too much, moments he'd nearly lost his nerve. But when it mattered most, he'd trusted the process. He'd done the right thing.

And he'd done it fifteen minutes from home. In his backyard. Just like the system said.

Before starting the car, he pulled out his phone and texted Mike Henderson.

Focus Day with Steve went great. He scheduled Vision Building. Wanted you to know—and to say thanks again for the intro. Meant the world.

The reply came within minutes: *So glad to hear it. He's a good guy. Let me know how it goes.*

That was the connector process. Keep them informed. Show appreciation. Make them feel like partners in the success, not just sources of leads. Alan added a note to his calendar: send Mike a gift in December.

His phone buzzed again. Robert.

How'd it go?

Alan thought for a moment, then typed his reply.

I almost played it safe. Glad I didn't. They scheduled Vision Building.

The response came immediately.

That's 1. Only 19 more to go.

Alan laughed out loud. He started the car and headed home. He'd be there in time for dinner with Sarah.

One down. Nineteen to go.

* * *

The following week, another opportunity emerged. But this one was different.

Derek Webb ran a manufacturing company in Cleveland. He'd heard about Alan through Mike Henderson, who had a connection to Derek's industry. Derek was eager to get started.

"I've been reading *Traction* for three weeks," Derek said during their introductory call. "I'm ready to go. When can you fly out?"

Cleveland. A twelve-hour drive or a two-hour flight.

Alan sat with the decision for two days. His backyard was Minneapolis. That's where he was supposed to build. Having only one local client didn't mean he should abandon the strategy.

But Derek was ready. And leads weren't exactly flowing in yet. The 4-2-1 system was working, but slowly. Four Warm Leads had turned into two 90-Minute Meetings. Steve was his only client so far.

That evening, he found Sarah in the kitchen and laid it out for her.

"Cleveland?" she said, setting down her tea. "That's not exactly your backyard."

"No. It's not."

"Help me understand what we're talking about here. What does taking this client actually mean?"

Alan pulled out a chair and sat down across from her. "Focus Day first. Then two Vision Building days, about a month apart. Then, quarterly sessions for as long as they're a client. Most clients stay two years. Some stay longer."

Sarah did the math. "So you're talking about flying to Cleveland every quarter for the next two years. Minimum."

"Yes."

"That's eight trips. At least. Could be more if they stay longer or if they need extra sessions."

"Yes."

"And each trip is what, two days? Three with travel?"

"Two if I'm efficient. Three if there are delays or if we run long."

Sarah was quiet for a moment. "You just sold your company so you could build something sustainable. Something local. Something that would give you more time with family, not less. And now you're talking about committing to quarterly travel to Ohio for the next two years of your life."

The words landed harder than Alan expected. She wasn't wrong.

"I know," he said. "But I need the reps. I need the confidence. I have one client, Sarah. One. And my pipeline is thin. What if Steve doesn't work out? What if the Minneapolis leads dry up? At least with Derek, I'd have a second client generating income while I build locally."

"That sounds like fear talking."

"Maybe it is. But the fear isn't irrational. I'm fifty-two years old, starting a new career from scratch. I can't afford to be precious about geography when someone is ready to write me a check."

Sarah picked up her tea again and took a slow sip. "What did they tell you at Boot Camp? About building in your backyard?"

Alan sighed. "That the goal is twenty clients you can serve without getting on a plane. That travel burns you out. That the best practices are built locally, through relationships and referrals that compound over time."

"And you're going to ignore that advice three weeks in?"

"I'm not ignoring it. I'm making an exception."

"One exception becomes two. Two becomes five. Before you know it, you're spending half your life in airports and hotel rooms, and you've built exactly the opposite of what you set out to build."

Alan rubbed his face with both hands. She was right. He knew she was right. But the fear was louder than the logic.

"What if I never get another local client?" he said quietly. "What if Steve was a fluke? What if I'm just not good enough to build a practice in my own backyard?"

Sarah reached across the table and took his hand. "That's head trash. You know that."

"Knowing it doesn't make it quieter."

They sat in silence for a long moment. The kitchen clock ticked. Outside, a car passed on the street.

"I'm not going to tell you what to do," Sarah finally said. "You're a grown man. You've built a company and sold it. You know how to make decisions." She paused. "But I want you to make this one with your eyes open. If you take Derek, you're committing to Cleveland for the next two years. That's two years of early morning flights. Two years of hotel rooms. Two years of missing dinners and soccer games and all the ordinary moments that add up to a life."

"I know."

"Do you? Because you just spent six years learning that the ordinary moments are the ones that matter. You missed so much when you were running RTS. You told me you'd never do that again."

Alan felt the weight of her words settle into his chest. She wasn't being dramatic. She was being honest. And the honesty hurt because it was true.

"I'm scared," he admitted. "I'm scared that if I say no to this, I'll regret it. I'm scared that I'll be sitting here six months from now with no clients and no income, wondering why I turned down a sure thing because of some principle about geography."

"And I'm scared that if you say yes, you'll be sitting in a Cleveland hotel room six months from now, missing Emily's graduation, wondering why you didn't trust yourself to build something real in your own city."

The silence stretched between them.

"What would you do?" Alan asked. "If you were me?"

Sarah shook her head. "That's not fair. I'm not you. I don't have your fear, but I also don't have your opportunity. Only you can decide what the right choice is."

Alan stared at the table. The fear and the principle, wrestling inside him. Twenty clients in your backyard. That was the system. That was the path to the EOS Life. But the system assumed you could get twenty clients in your backyard. What if you couldn't?

"I'm going to take it," he said finally. "I know all the reasons not to. I've heard them. I believe them. But I need this, Sarah. I need to know I can do this work. I need the income and the experience and the confidence. And right now, Marcus is the only one offering that."

Sarah nodded slowly. There was no judgment in her eyes, but there was something else. Resignation, maybe. Or sadness.

"Then take it," she said. "But promise me something."

"What?"

"Promise me you'll remember this conversation. When you're exhausted and frustrated and wondering why you're spending another night away from home, remember that you chose this. And remember what it costs."

"I will."

"And promise me that Cleveland stays an exception. One out-of-market client. Not two. Not five. One."

"I promise."

Sarah squeezed his hand, then let go. "Call Derek tomorrow. Tell him yes. And then come back to Minneapolis and build the practice you actually want."

* * *

The 90-Minute Meeting happened over video call the following week. Alan walked Derek and his leadership team through the same presentation he'd given Steve: the EOS Story, the About You questions, the Tools, and the Process. They were engaged from the start, leaning into their cameras, asking good questions, nodding at the right moments.

When Alan got to the fee presentation, he explained the travel rate.

"For clients outside my local market, my fee is six thousand dollars per session, plus travel expenses. That covers the additional time and the cost of being away from my backyard practice."

Derek didn't blink. "When can we start?"

They scheduled the Focus Day for three weeks out.

* * *

The Focus Day in Cleveland went well. Derek had a good team, and they were hungry for structure. Alan entered the danger when he needed to, facilitated cleanly, and earned his six-thousand-dollar check.

But on the flight home, watching the clouds pass beneath him, Sarah's words echoed in his mind.

Remember what it costs.

He'd be back in Cleveland in thirty days for Vision Building Day 1. And again, thirty days after that for Vision Building Day 2. And then quarterly, for as long as Derek stayed a client.

He'd made his choice. Now he had to live with it.

10

Finding His Rhythm

"Iron sharpens iron."

THE HIGH FROM Eden Prairie lasted exactly six days.

Alan returned home energized, certain that the momentum would carry him forward. He'd done it. He'd delivered a Focus Day. He'd entered the danger. He'd earned his first check. And Derek in Cleveland was already on the calendar. Two clients in his first month. The path was clear now. Then the local pipeline went dry.

Derek was great, but Derek was in Cleveland. Alan needed Minneapolis clients, the kind he could serve without getting on a plane. Week one back home, he made calls. Sent emails. Followed up with every contact on The List. Nothing. Week two, more of the same. By week three, the voice in his head had grown loud and insistent.

Maybe Steve was a fluke. Maybe you got lucky. Maybe you don't actually have what it takes to do this.

Head trash. That's what they called it at Boot Camp. The negative self-talk that creeps in when things get hard. The stories we tell ourselves about why we can't succeed.

Alan knew it was head trash. Knowing didn't make it quieter.

* * *

"You're spiraling," Robert said on their weekly call.

"I'm not spiraling. I'm being realistic."

"You're being dramatic. It's been three weeks."

"Three weeks with zero local Warm Leads. Zero Minneapolis 90-Minute Meetings. Derek's great, but I can't build a practice flying to Ohio."

"And how many coffees have you had?"

Alan paused. "What do you mean?"

"I mean, how many people have you actually sat down with? Face to face. Not emails. Not phone calls. Actual conversations where you listened to them talk about their business and their life for an hour."

The silence stretched.

"That's what I thought," Robert said. "You're working The List like it's a sales funnel. Names to call, boxes to check. But that's not how this works."

"Then how does it work?"

"It's 100 percent relational. Not transactional. You're not selling anything. You're building relationships. And you can't build relationships from behind a computer screen."

Alan thought about Don Tinney's story from Boot Camp. Don had started in Kalamazoo with no network, no resources, nothing but a belief in the system. He'd built his entire practice one coffee at a time, one conversation at a time, one relationship at a time.

"Start with the people who already know you," Robert continued. "Your friends. Your former colleagues. Your neighbors. Don't ask them for anything. Just tell them what you're doing. Share your excitement. Let them ask questions. And then ask them one thing: Who do you know that might benefit from hearing about this?"

"That's it?"

"That's it. But here's the key. Don't ask them to make an introduction. Don't put the burden on them. Ask if you can use their name when you reach out. That's all most people need. They want to help, but they don't want homework."

Alan grabbed a pen and started writing.

* * *

The next morning, Alan called Jim Hartley, a CFO he'd worked with years ago when RTS was bidding on a major contract. They'd stayed in touch over the years, grabbing lunch occasionally, trading referrals when it made sense. Jim had always respected Alan's business instincts.

"I've been wondering what you've been up to," Jim said. "Heard you sold RTS."

"I did. And then I did something crazy."

They met for coffee that afternoon. For the first thirty minutes, Alan just listened. Jim talked about his current company, his frustrations with leadership, and his concerns about the direction things were heading. Alan asked questions. He leaned in. He resisted every urge to jump in with solutions.

Finally, Jim asked, "So what are you doing now?"

Alan gave him the two-minute version. The VTH pitch he'd practiced hundreds of times, but delivered like a conversation, not a script.

Jim's eyes widened. "That's exactly what my CEO needs to hear. He's been hitting the ceiling for two years and doesn't know why."

"Do you think he'd be open to a conversation?"

"Absolutely. Can I give him your number?"

"Even better. I'll reach out to him directly. I'll just use your name and tell him you sent me, so he knows the connection."

Jim smiled and nodded. "Perfect. He'll appreciate that."

It was the same pattern that had worked with Mike Henderson. Help first. Listen. Give value. Then ask.

* * *

He learned to work The List differently after that.

Instead of treating it as a database to mine, he treated it as a map of relationships. Every name represented a person with their own network, their own connections, their own circle of business owners who might be frustrated, hitting the ceiling, or ready for help.

He subscribed to a professional networking tool that let him search for companies in the Twin Cities metro area by size and industry: 10 to 250 employees, privately held, the kinds of companies that fit the target market profile. Within days, he had a list of over two thousand potential prospects.

But the list itself was worthless. That was the insight that changed everything.

A name on a screen wasn't a Warm Lead. It was just data. A warm lead was a decision-maker who was willing to talk to him about EOS because someone they trusted had made the introduction. Without that trust, without that relationship, he was just another consultant cold-calling business owners who had gotten very good at fending off people who wanted their time.

So he used the tool differently. Instead of treating it as a prospecting list, he used it to understand his network's network. When he met someone for coffee, he could see which companies they were connected to. He could ask smarter questions. "I noticed you're connected to the owner of Midwest Manufacturing. How do you know them?"

He also brought a printed list of target companies to his coffee meetings.

"If you wouldn't mind," he'd say after explaining what he did, "could you look at this list and just mark any names you recognize? Anyone you know personally, anyone you've done business with, anyone whose owner you might have met at an event."

The first time he tried it, his contact marked three names. The second time, seven. The third time, twelve.

He never did the VTH pitch until he understood whether someone was truly a warm lead. A name wasn't enough. He needed to know: Does this person respect my connector's opinion? Would they take the call because of who made the introduction? If the answer wasn't a clear yes, he didn't reach out. He went back to building relationships instead.

By the end of his second month, Alan had twenty-three warm leads on his list. Not cold calls. Not random contacts. Real introductions from people who knew him and trusted him enough to lend their credibility.

The List became his obsession.

Every Sunday night, he sat at his desk and updated the spreadsheet they'd given him at Boot Camp. Company names in column B. Connector names in column C. First contact dates. Stages: A for active clients, B for prospects in the pipeline, C for warm leads not yet contacted, and D for future possibilities. He tracked every company's progression through the funnel: warm lead to 90-Minute Meeting to Focus Day to Vision Building. He knew his conversion rates cold. He could tell you which connectors were generating leads and which relationships needed more nurturing.

The Scorecard tab was where he measured his week: new warm leads generated, total warm leads and prospects in the pipeline, 90-Minute Meetings scheduled, Focus Days delivered, average client rating, days billed, and revenue collected. Every Monday morning, he updated the numbers before the community call.

The first time he got called on during a Monday Call, his heart nearly stopped.

"Alan Roth," the facilitator said. "You're three months in. Give us your numbers."

He unmuted his phone, suddenly aware of the hundred-plus Implementers listening. "Two new warm leads this week. Fourteen total in my pipeline. One 90-Minute Meeting scheduled for Thursday. One Focus Day completed last week, rating of nine. Revenue of four thousand."

"Good numbers for month three," the facilitator said. "What's your biggest challenge right now?"

"Converting warm leads to 90-Minute Meetings. I've got the relationships, but I'm struggling with the transition from coffee conversation to scheduling the actual meeting."

"Who's got advice for Alan?"

Three voices jumped in with suggestions. One Implementer shared a specific phrase she used. Another talked about the importance of timing. A third reminded him that not every warm lead was ready, and that was okay.

The whole exchange took ninety seconds. But Alan wrote down every word. This was why the Monday Calls mattered. A hundred people who'd been where he was, sharing what worked.

One afternoon, driving back from a coffee meeting in Edina, Alan found himself looking at the office parks and industrial buildings along I-494 with new eyes. Behind those walls were leadership teams hitting the ceiling, entrepreneurs lying awake at night, and companies that needed what he had to offer. Plymouth. Minnetonka. Bloomington. Eden Prairie. His backyard stretched thirty miles in every direction, and somewhere inside it were twenty clients waiting to be found. He just had to keep building relationships until he found them.

* * *

Not every lead converted.

His second 90-Minute Meeting was with a manufacturing company in St. Paul. The owner sat with his arms crossed the entire time, challenging every concept, questioning every tool. When Alan got to the fee presentation, the man laughed.

"Four thousand dollars for one day? I could hire a consultant for a month for that."

Alan felt his face flush. The head trash roared back. *He's right. Who do you think you are, charging that kind of money? You've done one Focus Day. One. You're not worth four thousand dollars.*

He thanked them for their time and left without scheduling anything.

That night, he called his coach, Maria.

"The fee objection hit you hard," she said after he'd explained what happened.

"It's not just the objection. It's that I think he might be right. Four thousand dollars for seven hours of work. That's almost six hundred dollars an hour. Who am I to charge that?"

Maria was quiet for a moment. "Let me tell you a story. You know Picasso?"

"The artist?"

"The artist. So the story goes that Picasso was sitting at a cafe in Paris when a woman approached him and asked if he would sketch her portrait. He agreed, and in just a few minutes, he drew her likeness on a napkin. When he handed it to her, she asked how much she owed him. He said ten thousand francs."

Alan waited.

"The woman was shocked. 'But it only took you five minutes!' she said. And Picasso replied, 'No, madam. It took me forty years and five minutes.'"

The words landed somewhere deep.

"You're not charging for seven hours," Maria continued. "You're charging for twenty years of building and running a business. You're charging for the transformation you went through with EOS. You're charging for the hundreds of hours you've spent mastering these tools. The session is the delivery mechanism, but the value is everything that came before it."

Alan thought about his years at RTS. The mistakes he'd made. The lessons he'd learned. The ceiling he'd hit and broken through. All of that was in the room with him when he facilitated a session. All of that was what he was really offering.

"The people who understand that will pay," Maria said. "The ones who don't aren't your clients. That's not rejection. That's selection."

* * *

His third 90-Minute Meeting converted. So did his fourth.

* * *

Month four brought his first QCE since Boot Camp.

Alan flew to Detroit for the Quarterly Collaborative Exchange, not knowing what to expect. Boot Camp had been intense but structured. This felt different. Looser. More like a gathering of old friends than a training event.

He recognized a few faces from his Boot Camp class. Others were strangers who somehow felt familiar. There was a shared language, a shared experience, a shared commitment to something bigger than any individual practice.

During the breakout session, Alan found himself in a small group with three Certified Implementers who had been doing this for years. He expected them to be guarded, competitive, protective of their secrets. Instead, they were generous to the point of absurdity.

"What's your biggest challenge right now?" one of them asked.

Alan hesitated. Admitting weakness to potential competitors felt dangerous.

"This is a safe space," another said, reading his hesitation. "We've all been where you are. Help first. That's not just a slogan. It's how we operate."

So Alan told them. The slow start in Minneapolis. The 90 that didn't convert. The head trash that kept telling him he wasn't good enough. He asked if they had any secrets, any tricks, any shortcuts he was missing.

The three Implementers exchanged a knowing glance.

"There are no silver bullets," one of them said. "I know that's not what you want to hear, but it's the truth. The answer is the 4-2-1 BizDev Checklist. Follow it religiously. Every week. Don't skip steps. Don't try to reinvent the wheel. Don't look for shortcuts that don't exist."

"That's it?"

"That's it. Four warm leads a month. Two 90-Minute Meetings. One new client. Do that consistently for eighteen months and you'll have a thriving practice. Try to find a faster way, and you'll waste time chasing tactics that don't work."

Another Implementer leaned in. "The first five clients are the hardest. Something clicks after five. The game slows down. You start getting referrals. You develop a credibility that you just can't manufacture. But you have to trust the process long enough to get there."

"How long did it take you to get to five?" Alan asked.

"Nine months. And I wanted to quit every single one of them."

Alan felt something shift in his chest. He wasn't alone. He wasn't broken. He was just on the path, the same path everyone else had walked. And the path wasn't complicated. It was just hard.

Two weeks after QCE, Alan's phone rang. The caller ID showed a name he barely recognized: Ryan Hollister, one of the Certified Implementers from the breakout session. They'd exchanged maybe ten sentences total.

"Alan, hey. Ryan Hollister. We met at QCE."

"Of course. Good to hear from you."

"Listen, I've got a situation. A business owner in Minneapolis reached out to me through a mutual contact. Great company, forty employees, classic hitting-the-ceiling scenario. They're ready to go." Greg paused. "But they're in your backyard, not mine. I'm in Milwaukee. I could take them, but it doesn't make sense. I want to refer them to you."

Alan was silent for a moment. In his old business world, leads were guarded like gold. You didn't hand them to someone you'd met once at a QCE.

"Why?" he finally asked.

Greg laughed. "Because that's how this works. Help first. If I hoard a lead that's better served by someone else, I'm not helping the client, and I'm not helping the community. Besides," he added, "EOS Worldwide policy is that you pay me fifty percent of the Focus Day. So I'm not exactly being selfless here. But honestly? I'd have sent you this referral even without that. It's the right thing to do."

Alan took down the details. The company was a perfect fit. Three weeks later, they became his fourth client.

He never forgot that call. In twenty-one years of business, no competitor had ever handed him an opportunity. Ryan Hollister barely knew him and had sent him a client anyway. That was the moment Alan truly understood what "Help First" meant. Not a slogan. Not a value on a wall. A way of operating that made everyone better.

* * *

By month six, Alan had five clients.

Derek in Cleveland was thriving. They'd completed Vision Building 1 and 2, and the transformation was remarkable. Dave had settled into his operations role with renewed energy. Derek hired an Integrator, a woman named Sandra, who brought exactly the structure and discipline the company needed. The quarterly sessions had become the highlight of Derek's calendar.

But the travel was taking its toll.

Every trip to Cleveland meant a 4:30 a.m. alarm. A rush to the airport. Two hours in a metal tube, followed by a rental car and a hotel room that looked like every other hotel room. The sessions themselves were good, sometimes great. But the margins around them were brutal.

He missed Emily's spring concert because of a Cleveland quarterly. Sarah had sent him a video, and he'd watched it in his hotel room that night, feeling the distance in a way he hadn't anticipated. She'd been right. He remembered their conversation in the kitchen, her warning about ordinary moments. He was living it now.

The worst part was the exhaustion. After a Cleveland trip, he needed a full day to recover. A day he could have spent on coffee meetings, connector calls, and building his Minneapolis practice. Instead, he'd sit in his home office, too tired to think clearly, watching his to-do list grow while his energy drained.

One client, he told himself. Just one out-of-market client. It won't derail everything.

But some nights, lying awake at 2 a.m. replaying the day's session in his head, too wired from travel and facilitation to sleep, he wondered if he'd made a mistake.

In Minneapolis, he'd added four more clients: a logistics company, a dental practice with three locations, a marketing agency, and a family-owned construction firm. Each one different. Each one teaching him something new about facilitation, about entering the danger, about trusting the room.

And each one, fifteen minutes from home.

The contrast was impossible to ignore. His Minneapolis clients felt sustainable. He could see them regularly, build real relationships, and be home for dinner. Cleveland felt like a tax he was paying for a decision made out of fear.

The head trash hadn't disappeared, but it had grown quieter. He was learning to recognize it for what it was: fear dressed up as wisdom. When it whispered that he wasn't good enough, he reminded himself of the clients who had scheduled their next sessions, the leaders who had thanked him with tears in their eyes, and the businesses that were actually changing because of the work they were doing together.

* * *

Robert called on a Tuesday evening, his voice lighter than usual.

"I have an idea."

"I'm listening."

"T-Group. You, me, and two others from our Boot Camp class. We meet every other week, hold each other accountable, and share what's working and what isn't. Iron sharpens iron."

"Who else?"

"Michelle from Phoenix and Jason from Atlanta. They're both in similar places. Five to seven clients, still figuring it out, hungry to get better."

Alan thought about the QCE breakout session, the power of having peers who understood the journey.

"I'm in."

Their first T-Group call lasted two hours. They shared their numbers. Their struggles. Their wins.

Michelle from Phoenix had the calm intensity of someone who'd worked in emergency rooms before starting her own healthcare consulting firm. She'd lost her first client, a company that decided EOS wasn't for them after Vision Building

2, and she was processing it with the clinical detachment of a surgeon reviewing a difficult case.

Derek from Atlanta was the opposite: emotional, animated, prone to dramatic hand gestures even on video. He was wrestling with a leadership team that wouldn't do their homework between sessions, and his frustration was palpable through the screen.

Robert approached his three consecutive 90-Minute conversations with the same methodical precision he'd brought to his logistics empire, trying to reverse-engineer what he'd done differently.

No one had all the answers. But together, they had more than any of them had alone.

The T-Group became a lifeline. Every other week, four faces on a video call, pushing each other to grow.

On their third call, Michelle admitted something she hadn't told anyone else.

"I'm scared to raise my fee," she said. "I know the math. I know I'm worth it. But every time I get to the fee presentation, I feel like a fraud."

"What's the story you're telling yourself?" Robert asked.

"That they'll laugh at me. That they'll say, 'Who do you think you are, charging that kind of money?'"

Alan leaned toward his camera. "Michelle, what happened the last time you quoted your full fee?"

"They paid it. Without blinking."

"And the time before that?"

"Same thing."

"So you've quoted your fee multiple times, clients have paid it happily, and you're still telling yourself they'll laugh at you?"

Michelle was quiet for a moment. "When you say it like that, it sounds ridiculous."

"It's not ridiculous," Derek said. "It's head trash. We all have it. The question is whether you're going to let it run your business or whether you're going to run your business despite it."

By the end of the call, Michelle had committed to raising her fee by five hundred dollars for her next new client. The group agreed to follow up in two weeks.

Before they signed off, Robert leaned back in his chair. "Can I share something? From my logistics days?"

"Please," Alan said.

"In shipping, everyone obsesses over the big moves. The container ships crossing oceans. The freight trains hauling thousands of tons. But you know where most deliveries fail?" He paused. "The last mile. The final stretch from the distribution center to someone's door. It's the shortest distance, but it's where everything breaks down. Packages get lost. Drivers get confused. Customers get frustrated."

Derek nodded slowly. "And this relates to us how?"

"We're in the last mile business," Robert said. "The EOS tools are the container ship. Gino built that. The training, the community, the system—that's the infrastructure. But we're the ones who have to deliver it to the door. And that last mile is where most people fail. Not because the system doesn't work. Because they don't trust the route." He looked at each of them through the screen. "Every time we deviate from the process—consult instead of facilitate, give answers instead of ask questions, skip a step because we think we know better— we're taking a wrong turn on the last mile. The package doesn't arrive. And we blame the system instead of our delivery."

The group was quiet for a moment.

"I'm writing that down," Michelle said.

Alan did too. *Trust the route.* It was the simplest summary of EOS purity he'd ever heard.

Alan hung up feeling something he hadn't expected: gratitude. Not just for the accountability, but for the permission to be imperfect. In his old life at RTS, he'd always had to project confidence, to have all the answers. Here, with these three people who understood the journey because they were walking it too, he could admit what he didn't know. He could ask for help. He could be human.

This was what iron sharpening iron looked like. Not advice from experts on high. Just honest questions from peers who cared enough to push.

11

The Fall

"Trust the route."

MONTH TEN BROUGHT Alan to his knees.

The client was a distribution company in Bloomington. The owner, Dana, had been enthusiastic throughout the 90-Minute Meeting and Focus Day. She reminded Alan of himself in the early RTS days: driven, impatient, certain she knew what her company needed. He'd seen the warning signs but ignored them. She was his ninth client. He was so close to the halfway mark.

The first Vision Building day started well enough. They worked through Core Values, and the team engaged. But when they got to the Accountability Chart, Dana started pushing back.

"I don't see why I can't be both Visionary and Integrator," she said. "I've been doing both for six years."

Alan knew the right answer. He'd taught it a dozen times. The two seats require different skill sets. Trying to fill both creates chaos. The company needs separation to scale.

But something shifted in him. Maybe it was Dana's confidence. Maybe it was his own desire to keep her happy. Maybe it was the voice whispering that he wasn't experienced enough to push back on someone who'd built a thirty-million-dollar company.

"Well," he heard himself say, "some founders do manage both roles. It's not ideal, but if you're committed to making it work, we can structure things to support that."

He watched Dana's face relax. The tension in the room eased. And in that moment, Alan felt something he hadn't felt since his consulting days: the hollow satisfaction of telling a client what they wanted to hear.

The rest of the session unraveled slowly. When the team struggled to agree on their 10-Year Target, Alan offered suggestions instead of facilitating. When they got stuck on the Marketing Strategy, he drew on his experience in the staffing industry and began consulting. "Here's what I've seen work," he said, filling the whiteboard with his ideas instead of theirs.

By the end of the day, Dana was pleased. "This was great," she said. "So much more practical than I expected."

Alan drove home with a check in his pocket and a pit in his stomach.

He knew what he'd done. He'd abandoned the process. He'd made it about his ideas instead of their answers. He'd given them a fish instead of teaching them to fish. Everything Sue had warned him about. Everything Boot Camp had drilled into him. He'd thrown it all away because he wanted to be liked.

The next week, Dana called to cancel Vision Building Day 2.

"We've decided to go a different direction," she said. "The session was helpful, but honestly, it felt more like consulting than what you described in our first meeting. We can find consultants for a lot less than your fee."

Alan tried to respond, but the words caught in his throat.

"We'll send the check for VB1," Dana continued. "But we won't be continuing."

After she hung up, Alan sat at his desk for a long time. The head trash wasn't whispering anymore. It was screaming. *You're a fraud. You don't have what it takes. You abandoned everything you believe in because you were scared to push back. Sue would be ashamed. The community would be ashamed. You should be ashamed.*

He didn't tell Sarah that night. He made small talk over dinner, helped Emily with her homework, and went through the motions of normalcy. The meatloaf tasted like cardboard. Everything did. After Sarah went to bed, he found himself in the living room, sitting in the dark, staring at nothing.

That's where she found him at midnight.

"Alan?" Sarah's voice was soft, concerned. She sat down next to him on the couch. "What's wrong?"

He couldn't look at her. "I lost a client today."

"That happens. You've said it yourself. Not every company is ready."

"This was different." His voice cracked. "I didn't lose them because they weren't ready. I lost them because I wasn't ready. I abandoned everything I'm supposed to stand for. I was consulting instead of teaching, coaching, and facilitating. I gave them my answers instead of helping them find theirs." He finally looked at her. "I was a fraud, Sarah. And they saw right through me."

Sarah was quiet for a moment. "Why did you do it?"

"Because I wanted her to like me. Because I was scared that if I pushed back, she'd fire me on the spot. Because part of me still doesn't believe I have the right to challenge someone who's built more than I ever did." He laughed bitterly. "Twenty-one years of running a company, and I still can't get out of my own way."

"So what are you going to do?"

Alan shook his head. "I don't know. Maybe this was a mistake. Maybe I'm not cut out for this."

Sarah took his hand. "Do you remember what you told me after your first session with Sue? After the Focus Day, when everything changed for RTS?"

He didn't respond.

"You said it was the first time anyone had ever told you the truth about your business. Not what you wanted to hear. What you needed to hear. You said that's what made it different from every consultant you'd ever hired."

Alan closed his eyes. He remembered. The way Sue had pushed back when he'd tried to stay in the Integrator seat. The way she'd called out the dysfunction on his leadership team. The way she'd refused to give him easy answers, even when he begged for them.

"You became an Implementer to give that gift to other people," Sarah continued. "Not to be liked. Not to be comfortable. To help them see what they can't see themselves." She squeezed his hand. "You can't do that if you're trying to make them happy. You can only do it if you're willing to make them better."

Alan sat with that for a long time. The house was silent around them. The weight of his failure pressed down on his chest.

"I have to call her," he finally said.

"Dana?"

"No. My coach. Maria. I have to tell her what happened. All of it." He took a breath. "And then I have to figure out how to make sure it never happens again."

Sarah leaned her head on his shoulder. "That's the Alan I married. The one who doesn't run from hard things."

He didn't sleep that night. But somewhere in the dark hours, something shifted. The shame didn't disappear, but it transformed into something else. Resolve. Clarity. A bone-deep understanding of what he'd almost thrown away.

Robert's words from their T-Group meeting haunted him. *Trust the route. Every time we deviate from the process, we're taking a wrong turn on the last mile. The package doesn't arrive.*

Alan hadn't trusted the route. He'd taken the wrong turn. And now he had to find his way back.

He called Maria at seven the next morning.

"I need to tell you about a session that went wrong," he said. "And I need you to help me understand why I let it happen."

The conversation lasted two hours. Maria didn't let him off the hook. She pushed him to examine every moment where he'd compromised, every choice that had led him away from the process. It was brutal. It was necessary.

"You discovered something important," she said at the end. "You learned what kind of Implementer you don't want to be. That's valuable. The question is whether you're going to use it."

"I am," Alan said. "I have to."

"Then here's your homework. Before your next session, I want you to write down the three moments when you're most tempted to consult instead of teach, coach, and facilitate. The three situations where you feel the pull to give answers instead of ask questions. Know your danger zones. Because now you know what happens when you don't."

Alan wrote them down that afternoon. Clients who intimidate him. Moments of team conflict. Silences that feel uncomfortable.

He taped the list to his desk, where he could see it before every session.

* * *

Month twelve brought a crisis.

Alan had been working with the construction company for six months. The owner, a man named Frank, had been enthusiastic at first. He'd embraced the tools, done the homework, and pushed his leadership team to engage. But somewhere around the third quarterly session, something shifted.

The team started showing up unprepared. Rocks were incomplete. Scorecard numbers were missing. The Level 10 Meetings had devolved into complaint sessions. And Frank, who had once been Alan's biggest champion, had grown distant and defensive.

"I don't think this is working," Frank said at the start of their fourth quarterly.

Alan felt his stomach drop. "Tell me more."

"We're doing all this work, all these sessions, and nothing's really changing. My people are still frustrating me. We're still missing deadlines. I'm still working sixty hours a week."

The room was silent. The other leaders stared at the table, unwilling to make eye contact.

Alan knew what he was supposed to do. Enter the danger. Say the hard thing. But the head trash was screaming now. *This is your fault. You didn't implement it correctly. You're going to lose this client, and everyone will know you failed.*

He took a breath. Remembered the Core Values. Do the Right Thing. No amount of money is worth betraying a trust.

"Frank," Alan said slowly, "can I be direct with you?"

Frank nodded, his jaw tight.

"I think you're right that something isn't working. But I don't think it's the system. I think it's the implementation. And I think that starts with leadership."

The room went colder.

"The tools only work if the leadership team models them. If you're not doing your Rocks, your people won't do their Rocks. If you're not coming to sessions prepared, they won't come prepared. If you're not holding them accountable, they'll learn that accountability is optional."

Frank's face reddened. "Are you saying this is my fault?"

"I'm saying the fish rots from the head. That's not blame. That's just how organizations work. The leadership team sets the tone. Always."

For a long moment, Alan was certain he was about to be fired. He'd pushed too hard. Said too much. Lost the client and proven that his head trash was right all along.

Then Frank's shoulders dropped.

"You're not wrong," he said quietly. "I've been phoning it in. I got excited about the tools, and then I got frustrated when they didn't fix everything overnight." He looked around the table at his team. "I haven't been showing up the way I need to. And that's on me."

The session that followed was the most productive they'd ever had. Frank recommitted to the process. The team recommitted to each other. They rebuilt their Rocks with real accountability. They identified the issues they'd been avoiding and actually IDSed them.

At the end of the day, Frank shook Alan's hand.

"That was hard to hear. But it was exactly what I needed. Thank you for having the guts to say it."

Alan drove home that night with a new understanding. The danger wasn't just something to fall into when things went wrong. It was the difference between being a facilitator who helped teams feel good and being an Implementer who helped teams get better. Sometimes helping meant saying the hard thing. And saying the hard thing required believing that you had something worth saying.

* * *

By month eighteen, Alan had twelve clients.

The 4-2-1 system was working. Four warm leads a month, two 90-Minute Meetings, and one new client. Some months were better, some worse, but the average held. His calendar was filling. His confidence was growing. The head trash still surfaced occasionally, but it no longer controlled him.

He'd raised his fee to $4,500. Then $5,000. Each increase felt terrifying until it didn't. The clients who valued the work paid without complaint. The ones who balked probably weren't the right fit anyway.

His T-Group had become essential. Every other week, four Implementers on a video call, pushing each other to grow, holding each other accountable, celebrating wins, and processing losses. Iron sharpening iron, just as the community promised.

He'd attended four QCEs now. Each one filled him with something he hadn't expected: gratitude. Gratitude for the system that worked. Gratitude for the community that supported him. Gratitude for the chance to do work that actually mattered.

One evening, Sarah found him at the kitchen table, reviewing his client list.

"You look different," she said.

"Different how?"

"Lighter. Like you're not carrying the weight of the world anymore."

Alan thought about it. She was right. At RTS, even on the good days, there had been a constant pressure. The responsibility of employees. The fear of failure. The sense that everything depended on him and him alone.

Now the weight was different. He still worked hard. He still worried. But the worry was productive, not paralyzing. And for the first time in his career, he felt like he was doing exactly what he was supposed to be doing.

"I'm getting close," he said.

"Close to what?"

"Twenty clients. That's the milestone. Twenty clients, a hundred sessions, and you're on track for the kind of practice that can sustain a real life. Not just a business. A life."

Sarah sat down across from him. "And then what?"

Alan smiled. "Then I keep going. The path to mastery has no destination. But I'm finally on it. And I'm not planning to stop."

Eight more clients. Eight more leadership teams to help. Eight more companies to transform.

12

The EOS Life

"Go deeper, not wider."

YEAR THREE BEGAN with a celebration.

Alan had hit the milestone. Twenty clients. Over a hundred sessions delivered. His fee had climbed to $5,500, and clients were paying it without hesitation. The referrals were flowing. His calendar was full. His T-Group had become a lifeline, four Implementers pushing each other toward mastery every other week.

He remembered what Sue had told him over lunch at that hotel bar, back when this had all seemed like a fantasy. *Twenty clients within about three years. A hundred sessions at four thousand each. The four hundred thousand dollar system.* He'd done the math back then and wondered if it was too good to be true.

Now, at $5,500 per session, he'd exceeded the promise. The system worked. It actually worked.

He'd done it. He'd actually done it.

At the QCE that spring, a Certified Implementer pulled him aside after a breakout session.

"You're one of the ones who's going to make it," she said. "I can tell. You've got the hunger. You've got the discipline. Just don't let success go to your head."

Alan smiled and thanked her for the kind words. But privately, he dismissed the warning. He wasn't the type to get cocky. He was too grounded for that. Too humble.

At least, that's what he told himself.

* * *

The slide started so gradually that he didn't notice it.

With twenty-one clients on his roster and a waiting list forming, Alan began to feel like he'd cracked the code. The 4-2-1 BizDev Checklist that had saved him in the early days now felt unnecessary. He was getting referrals without trying. Clients were coming to him. Why spend time on coffee meetings and connector calls when the business was already thriving?

He stopped updating The List. He skipped the Monday Calls. His weekly business development activities, once sacrosanct, became sporadic, then rare, then nonexistent.

"I've graduated from that phase," he told Robert during one of their T-Group calls. "The checklist is for people who are still building. I'm maintaining now."

Robert was quiet for a moment. "Are you sure about that? Remember what they taught us at Boot Camp. Focus compounds. Distraction dissipates."

"That was about building. I've built. Now I'm coasting."

"There's no coasting in this work, Alan. You're either moving forward, or you're sliding back."

Alan waved off the concern. "Look at my numbers. Twenty-one clients. Full calendar. I'm exactly where I wanted to be."

"And what happens when some of those clients graduate? Or get acquired? Or just decide they're done?"

"I've got a waiting list. I'll be fine."

He wasn't fine.

* * *

The first client to leave was Derek.

After three years together, Derek's company had transformed. They'd found their Integrator. They'd built their leadership team. They'd systematized their processes and created a Meeting Pulse that ran like clockwork. In their final quarterly session, Derek shook Alan's hand and said the words every Implementer dreams of hearing.

"We don't need you anymore. You've worked yourself out of a job."

It was exactly what was supposed to happen. Alan had always known that the goal was to create independence, not dependence. But losing Derek still stung. He'd been Alan's second client, his first out-of-market risk.

Three years. Twelve quarterly trips to Cleveland. Thirty-six nights in hotel rooms, not counting the Vision Building days. Alan had kept his promise to Sarah, technically. One out-of-market client, not two. But one client for three years had cost him more than he'd ever anticipated. The 4 a.m. alarms. The missed family dinners. The exhaustion that followed every trip. The coffee meetings he'd skipped because he was too tired to be present.

Sarah had been right that night in the kitchen. She'd told him to remember what it costs. Now, watching Derek's company graduate, he finally understood the full price.

The work had been good. Derek's transformation was real. But if Alan could go back and do it again, he'd have said no. He'd have trusted his backyard, trusted the system, trusted that Minneapolis had enough entrepreneurs who needed help.

Some lessons you can only learn the hard way.

Over the next six months, four more clients graduated. Two others were acquired by larger companies that already had their own systems in place. One simply decided that EOS wasn't for them anymore and walked away.

Alan watched his client count drop from twenty-one to fourteen. Then twelve.

His calendar, once overflowing, now had gaps. His income, once climbing steadily, plateaued and then declined. And his pipeline, neglected for nearly a year, was empty.

The head trash came roaring back.

You got lucky. You caught a wave, and now it's over. You were never as good as you thought you were.

He tried to restart the 4-2-1 process, but his connectors had gone cold. His network had atrophied. The relationships he'd spent two years building had withered from neglect. Rebuilding them would take months, maybe longer.

Months he wasn't sure he had.

* * *

The lifeline came from an unexpected place.

At a networking event, Alan met Vanessa Marshall, who ran a sales training company. She proposed a partnership: Alan would get certified in her methodology and deliver training to EOS clients and referrals.

It sounded logical. A way to diversify revenue and fill calendar gaps. Within two months, Alan was delivering sales workshops. Within three months, he had five sales consulting clients in addition to his twelve EOS clients.

He was busier than ever. He was making money again.

He was also miserable.

And something else gnawed at him. When he'd gone through Boot Camp, they'd been clear about EOS purity: the trust relationship depended on clients knowing their Implementer was there to implement EOS, period. Not to cross-sell. Not to use the relationship as a gateway to other revenue. The moment an

Implementer started cross-selling, clients would start wondering if that recommendation was truly in their best interest.

Every time he mentioned Vanessa's methodology to an EOS client, he felt a twinge of discomfort. He was eroding the very trust that made EOS implementation work.

He pushed the feeling aside. He had bills to pay and didn't want to tap into his savings from the sale of RTS. That was for retirement. And he hated it when cash was going in the wrong direction.

Or so he told himself.

* * *

The problem wasn't that the sales training was bad. Vanessa's methodology was solid. The problem was that Alan wasn't good at it.

He could deliver the content. But he didn't have the depth, the mastery, the instinctive understanding that came from years of living inside a system. When clients asked questions beyond the curriculum, he fumbled.

Worse, the sales work was cannibalizing his EOS practice. Every day he spent on sales training was a day he wasn't building relationships for EOS. Every hour preparing for a sales workshop was an hour he wasn't mastering the tools he was supposed to be teaching.

His EOS sessions started to suffer. His session ratings, once consistently above 9, dipped to 8.5. Then 8.2. One client rated a quarterly session at 7.8, and Alan couldn't honestly say they were wrong.

He was spreading himself thin, and everyone could see it except him.

The moment of clarity came during a sales workshop in St. Paul.

Alan stood at the whiteboard, teaching Vanessa's methodology to a group of twelve salespeople. His hand moved mechanically through the familiar diagrams. His voice delivered the content with professional polish. But inside, he felt hollow.

"What if the prospect says they need to think about it?" one participant asked.

Alan gave the scripted answer. It was a good answer. Vanessa's methodology was solid. But as the words left his mouth, he felt like an actor reading someone else's lines. He glanced at the clock. Two more hours. He found himself wishing he were facilitating an IDS session instead, watching a leadership team break through to a real solution, feeling the energy shift when someone finally named the elephant in the room.

During the lunch break, Alan sat alone in the corner of the training room, picking at a sandwich he didn't want. He pulled out his phone and scrolled through his EOS client list. Sixteen names. Sixteen companies he was supposed to be helping transform. When was the last time he'd really been present for any of them?

He thought about Sue Hawkes. About the way Sue had always seemed fully there, completely engaged, as if each session was the most important thing in the world. Alan couldn't remember the last time he'd felt that way about anything.

The afternoon session dragged. Alan delivered the content, answered the questions, and earned his fee. But driving home that evening, he couldn't shake the feeling that he'd spent the day doing something that didn't matter. Not to him. Not really.

* * *

The call came on a Tuesday afternoon.

"Alan, this is CJ Dubé. I don't think we've met, but I've been in the EOS community for a long time. I was a Community Leader before I stepped back to focus on my own practice."

Alan knew the name. CJ was a legend in the Implementer world, one of the early adopters who had helped shape the community's culture.

"I've been hearing things," CJ continued. "From other Implementers, from people at QCEs. They're worried about you."

Alan felt his defenses rise. "Worried about what?"

"They say you've been doing sales consulting. That you've been spreading yourself across multiple service lines. That your EOS work has been suffering."

"I'm just diversifying. Building a more sustainable business model."

"Is that what you're telling yourself?"

The directness caught Alan off guard. He'd forgotten how Implementers talked to each other. No dancing around the issue. No softening the blow. Just the truth, delivered straight.

"Let me ask you something," CJ said. "When you're in a sales training session, do you feel the same energy you feel in an EOS session? Do you light up the same way? Do you lose track of time because you're so immersed in helping them?"

Alan didn't answer. He didn't need to.

"Here's what I've learned in my years doing this," CJ continued. "EOS is a low-inertia system. Do you know what that means?"

"I'm not sure."

"It means that momentum matters. When you consistently do the 4-2-1 checklist, build relationships, and stay connected to your network, the flywheel spins faster and faster. Referrals come. Clients stay. Growth compounds. But the moment you stop pushing, the wheel starts to slow. And it slows faster than you'd expect."

Alan thought about his empty pipeline. His neglected connectors. The year he'd spent coasting on momentum, he hadn't realized was finite.

"You stopped pushing," CJ said. "And now you're trying to make up the difference with sales consulting. But here's the truth, Alan. You're robbing your sales clients of a masterful sales coach. And you're robbing your EOS clients of a masterful EOS Implementer. You can't be masterful at both. Nobody can."

"So what am I supposed to do? My client count is down. I need the revenue."

"You need to get back to basics. The 4-2-1 checklist works. It always works. But you have to trust it enough to do it consistently, even when things are going well. Especially when things are going well."

"That could take months to rebuild."

"It might. But here's something else you should know. When you have more leads than you can handle, you don't have to turn them away. You refer them to other Implementers. You stay abundance-minded. You help them find the right fit, and in return, you build trust and respect in the community. Other Implementers will do the same for you. That's how this works. That's how you stay balanced without losing your practice."

Alan was quiet for a long moment.

"Let the sales experts do sales," CJ said. "Let the other coaches and consultants do what they do. You're an EOS Implementer on the path to mastery. Stay on that path. Go deeper, not wider. Your clients deserve a master, not a generalist."

She paused, and when she spoke again, her voice was gentler but no less direct.

"There's something else, Alan. And I think you already know this, even if you haven't wanted to admit it. When you start selling other services to your EOS clients, you're compromising the trust relationship. The whole system depends on clients knowing that we're there to help them implement EOS. That's it. The moment they start wondering if our recommendations are about their best interest or our revenue, we've lost something we can never fully get back."

Alan closed his eyes. She was right. He'd known it all along.

"EOS purity isn't just about delivering the tools correctly," CJ continued. "It's about protecting the integrity of the relationship. EOS Worldwide, the Implementer community, and every client we serve are all connected by trust. When one Implementer erodes that trust, it affects all of us."

"What if I can't get back to where I was?"

"You can. The system works. But you have to work the system. Every week. Every month. No shortcuts. No coasting. The path to mastery has no destination, remember? You're either moving forward or you're sliding back. There's no standing still."

* * *

Alan ended the sales consulting arrangement the following week.

Vanessa was disappointed but understanding. She'd sensed for a while that his heart wasn't in it. They parted on good terms, with Alan referring her to several contacts who might benefit from her training.

Then he went back to the beginning.

He pulled out the 4-2-1 BizDev Checklist and started over. Coffee meetings. Connector calls. Updating The List. Mailing *Traction* books to prospects. All the unglamorous work he'd convinced himself he'd outgrown.

Robert's words from their first T-Group meeting echoed in his mind: *Trust the route.* Every time we deviate from the process, we're taking a wrong turn on the last mile. The package doesn't arrive.

Alan had taken a lot of wrong turns. Now he was finding his way back to the route.

It was humbling. After three years as a successful Implementer, he was essentially rebuilding his practice from scratch. But this time, he understood something he hadn't grasped before. The checklist wasn't training wheels to be discarded once you learned to ride. It was the bicycle itself. Without it, you weren't going anywhere.

The first month was brutal. Old connectors had moved on or forgotten him. New relationships took time to build. His calendar stayed sparse.

The second month was better. A few warm leads emerged. A 90-Minute Meeting converted. One new client.

By the third month, the flywheel had started spinning again. Referrals trickled in. His session ratings climbed back above 9. He felt the familiar energy returning, the sense that he was doing exactly what he was meant to do.

* * *

The mastery moment came unexpectedly, during a Quarterly with his logistics client.

Alan walked into the session and immediately sensed something was wrong. The team was going through the motions. Scorecard numbers were green. Rocks were on track. But there was an elephant in the room that no one was naming.

During the Issues List, Alan watched the team carefully. The CEO, a man named Howard, kept glancing at his CFO, Sandra. Sandra kept her eyes fixed on her notes. The other leaders shifted uncomfortably whenever finance came up.

When the team prioritized their top three issues, none of them touched on what was really going on.

Alan set down his marker.

"Before we IDS these," he said, "I need to name something. There's an issue in this room that nobody's willing to put on the list. I can feel it. I've been watching you for the last two hours, and something's off."

The room went cold.

"Howard," Alan said, "what's really going on between you and Sandra?"

Howard's face reddened. Sandra looked like she wanted to disappear.

The silence stretched for what felt like minutes. Then Howard spoke.

"Sandra gave her notice last week. She's leaving for a competitor. We've been trying to figure out how to tell the team."

The next hour was uncomfortable, honest, and ultimately healing. The team processed the news together. They discussed transition plans. They discovered an opportunity they hadn't seen: one of Sandra's direct reports had been ready for more responsibility for months. By the end of the session, they had a succession plan, a timeline, and something they hadn't had when they walked in: clarity.

At the end of the session, Howard shook Alan's hand.

"How did you know?"

"I didn't know," Alan said. "I just knew something wasn't being said. The answer is always in the room. Sometimes you just have to make space for it."

Driving home that evening, Alan realized he'd done something he couldn't have done two years ago. He'd entered a danger he couldn't see, trusted his instincts, and helped a team break through a barrier they hadn't even named.

That was mastery. Not knowing all the answers. Just being present enough to ask the right questions.

* * *

Six months after CJ's call, Alan sat in his home office reviewing his client list.

Sixteen clients. Not twenty-one, but growing. His pipeline was healthy again, with eight warm leads at various stages. He'd raised his fee to $6,000 for new clients, and no one had balked.

A LinkedIn notification popped up on his screen. He clicked it and smiled. Lauren had just been promoted to VP of Operations at the company that acquired RTS. She'd posted a photo of herself with her new team, captioned: "Grateful for the leaders who taught me what accountability really looks like. You know who you are." Alan liked the post and moved on, but the warmth lingered. His people had landed well. That mattered more than he'd expected.

More importantly, he'd found a rhythm he could sustain.

He glanced at the V/TO pinned to the corkboard above his desk—his own V/TO, for his own practice. He'd built it during Boot Camp, just like everyone else in his class, feeling slightly foolish applying the tools to a one-person business. But it worked. His 10-Year Target: be recognized as one of the top EOS Implementers in Minnesota, having helped 100+ companies transform. His 3-Year Picture: twenty clients, $500K in revenue, a waiting list of referrals, and home for dinner every night. He was on track. The same tools he taught his clients were running his own life.

He was doing the checklist every week, building relationships, and staying connected to his network. But he was also protecting his time, saying no to opportunities that didn't fit, referring excess leads to other Implementers rather than trying to serve everyone himself.

When a potential client in Denver had reached out, Alan had connected her with an Implementer in Colorado who was a better geographic fit. When a manufacturing company wanted help with issues outside the EOS wheelhouse, he'd referred them to specialists who could actually help. Each referral strengthened his relationships in the community. Each "no" created space for a better "yes."

Sarah found him at his desk one evening, staring out the window at the autumn leaves.

"You seem peaceful," she said.

"I think I finally understand what they meant by The EOS Life."

"Which is?"

Alan smiled. "Doing what you love. With people you love. Making a huge difference. Being compensated appropriately. And having time for other passions." He paused. "I was so focused on the compensated appropriately part that I almost lost everything else."

"And now?"

"Now I've got seventeen clients who are transforming their businesses. I've got a T-Group that pushes me to grow every week. I've got a community that has my back. I'm making more money than I did at RTS and working fewer hours. And I'm home for dinner every night."

Sarah sat down across from him. "That's quite a list."

"It's not a list," Alan said. "It's a life. The life I was trying to find when I walked away from RTS. I just didn't know how to build it. I had to learn." He laughed quietly. "And then I had to learn it again after I forgot."

"Will you forget again?"

Alan thought about it. "Probably. That's why the system matters. It's not about being perfect. It's about having something to come back to when you drift. The checklist. The community. The path." He looked at Sarah. "And you. You're the most important part of the system."

She reached across the desk and took his hand.

"So what's next?" she asked.

"More of the same. Deeper, not wider. Mastery, not expansion. And in two weeks, I've got a 90-Minute Meeting with a company that was referred by Derek. They're right here in Minneapolis. Apparently, he tells everyone about his EOS Implementer."

"The one in Cleveland?"

"The one in Cleveland. Turns out he's become one of my best connectors, even from eight hours away." Alan shook his head with a rueful smile. "The irony isn't lost on me. Three years of travel to Cleveland, and the referrals he sends are all local. If I'd been patient, I might have gotten those referrals anyway, without ever getting on a plane."

Sarah smiled. "Some lessons take a while to sink in."

"They do." Alan squeezed her hand. "But I finally learned this one. Twenty clients in my backyard. No exceptions. No matter how ready someone in Cleveland or Phoenix or Atlanta says they are." He paused. "Help first. Build relationships. Trust the process. Stay humble. And never, ever stop doing the checklist."

The path to mastery had no destination. But for the first time, Alan wasn't trying to reach one. He was just walking. One step at a time. One client at a time. One week at a time.

And that, he was finally learning, was enough.

EPILOGUE

The Call

"The path to mastery has no destination."

THE PHONE RANG on a Thursday afternoon.

Alan was in his home office, reviewing his prep notes for a quarterly session the following week. The client was a dental practice with three locations, one of his earliest Minneapolis wins. They'd been running on EOS for years now, and the transformation had been remarkable. Three practices operating as one company, with clear accountability, aligned vision, and a leadership team that actually functioned as a team.

He glanced at the caller ID. Unknown number, Minneapolis area code.

"This is Alan Roth."

"Alan, this is John Fredrickson. You don't know me, but I got your card from Eileen Sharp. She said I should call you."

Alan leaned back in his chair and smiled. Eileen. It had been a few months since they'd talked. Swan Services had graduated from his process over a year ago, and Eileen was running her own quarterly sessions now. She'd become exactly the kind of leader he'd hoped she would be: confident, capable, and generous with referrals.

"John, thanks for calling. Eileen mentioned you might reach out. How are you?"

There was a pause on the other end. When John spoke again, his voice carried the familiar weight of frustration that Alan had heard hundreds of times before.

"Honestly? I've been better."

"Tell me more."

And John did. He talked about building his construction business from scratch over eleven years. About the first eight years being fun and the last three being brutal. About working seventy hours a week and lying awake at night worrying about problems he hadn't had time to fix during the day. About cycling through internal promotions and external hires and consultants, none of whom had made a lasting difference.

"I know it's my fault," John said. "In this condition, I can't be an easy guy to work for. Honestly, Alan, if I can't figure this out, I'm going to sell the damn company and start over."

Alan listened without interrupting. He'd learned long ago that the most powerful thing he could do in these moments was simply be present. Let the entrepreneur pour out what they'd been carrying. Honor the weight of it before offering anything in return.

"John," Alan said when the silence settled, "I appreciate you sharing all of that with me. It sounds like you've hit the ceiling."

"The ceiling?"

"It's a concept in the system I use. Every entrepreneur hits the ceiling at some point. The things that got you here won't get you there. The skills, the habits, the approaches that built a successful business start to work against you when the business outgrows them."

"That's exactly what it feels like," John said. "Like everything that used to work just... doesn't anymore."

"And yet the harder you push, the worse it gets."

"Yes." John's voice cracked slightly. "How do you know that?"

"Because I've been there myself. And because I've worked with hundreds of entrepreneurs who were in the same place you are right now."

"How do you help them?" John asked.

Alan felt the familiar rhythm of the warm call settle over him. The same words Sue had used with him, all those years ago.

"I help entrepreneurs get what they want from their businesses. I do that by providing a complete system with simple, real-world, practical tools to help you and your leadership team do three things we call vision, traction, and healthy."

He paused, letting the words land.

"Vision, from the standpoint of getting your leaders 100 percent on the same page with where your organization is going and how it's going to get there. Traction, which means helping your leaders become more disciplined and accountable, executing really well to achieve every part of your vision. And healthy, meaning helping your leaders become a healthy, functional, cohesive leadership team. Because, unfortunately, leaders often don't function well as a team."

"That sounds like us," John admitted.

"From there, as goes your leadership team, so goes the rest of your organization. We get to the point where your entire organization is crystal clear on your vision, all much more disciplined and accountable, executing well, gaining consistent traction, and advancing as a healthy, functional, cohesive team."

"Eileen said you're different from other consultants," John said carefully.

"I don't call myself a consultant. I'm an Implementer. The difference is that I'm not here to tell you what to do or to do it for you. I'm here to help you and your leadership team master a system that you'll run yourselves. My job is to work myself out of a job."

"That's a strange business model."

Alan laughed. "It works better than you'd think. When clients succeed, they tell other people. That's how I got your number."

John was quiet for a moment. "So what's the next step?"

"I'd like to give you and your leadership team ninety minutes of my time. No charge, no obligation. Afterward, you'll all be fully equipped to decide whether there's a fit."

"Ninety minutes?"

"Ninety minutes. I call it the 90-Minute Meeting. I'll walk you through the system, show you how it works, and answer all your questions. If you decide to move forward, great. If not, you'll still walk away with some valuable insights about your business."

"And if we do decide to move forward?"

"Then we schedule a Focus Day, and your transformation begins."

They talked logistics for a few more minutes. John's leadership team consisted of five people, including himself. Alan suggested they find a date when everyone could commit to being present and fully engaged for the full ninety minutes. No phones. No interruptions. No one ducking out early.

"One more thing," Alan said before they hung up. "Before the meeting, I'd like you to think about one question: What do you really want from your business?"

"What do you mean?"

"Most entrepreneurs I work with started their companies because they wanted something. Freedom. Wealth. Impact. The chance to build something meaningful. Somewhere along the way, the business became a prison instead of a vehicle. I want to help you remember what you were building toward in the first place."

John was silent for a long moment.

"I'll think about that," he said finally. "Thank you, Alan."

"Thank you for calling, John. I'm looking forward to meeting you and your team."

* * *

After hanging up, Alan sat quietly in his office, letting the conversation settle.

Ten years ago, he'd been where John was now. Frustrated. Exhausted. Certain that something was broken but unable to see what it was. He'd hit his own ceiling at RTS and couldn't find a way through.

Then Sue Hawkes had handed him a book called *Traction*, and everything had changed.

Sue was fully Emeritus now, living in Arizona, down to just two clients she couldn't bear to let go. They still talked a few times a year. When Alan had hit the twenty-client milestone, he'd called to tell her. "You did it," she'd said, and he could hear the smile in her voice. "I knew you would." It meant more than any certification or client testimonial ever could. The woman who'd started it all, who'd seen something in him before he'd seen it in himself, knew that he'd become what she'd hoped he could be.

But Sue wasn't really where it had started. It had started with Paul Harrison, sliding a napkin across a table at a Roundtable meeting, telling Alan to call a woman who could help. Paul had no idea that his simple act of generosity would change Alan's entire life. That was the thing about Help First. You never knew which small gift would become someone else's turning point.

Now he was on the other side. Not as someone who had figured everything out, but as someone who had found a path and learned to walk it. A path that had led him through his own transformation, through Boot Camp, through his first client in Eden Prairie, through the struggles and stumbles and lessons of building a practice from nothing.

The path to mastery has no destination.

He understood that now in a way he couldn't have understood it at the beginning. Mastery wasn't a place you arrived. It was a way you traveled. Every client taught him something. Every session deepened his understanding. Every challenge revealed something new about the tools, about himself, about the infinite complexity of helping human beings work together effectively.

He thought about John Fredrickson, sitting in his office right now, probably wondering if he'd made a mistake by calling. Wondering if this Alan Roth character was just another consultant with a slick pitch and an empty promise.

Alan smiled. He'd felt that same skepticism when he first heard about EOS. He'd dismissed it as too simple, too structured, too good to be true. Even after he decided to reach out, it had taken him time to realize that simple wasn't the same as easy, and structure wasn't the same as constraint.

In two weeks, he'd sit down with John and his team. He'd walk them through the system the same way he'd walked hundreds of teams through it. He'd watch their faces shift from skepticism to curiosity to hope. He'd answer their questions, address their concerns, and give them everything they needed to make an informed decision.

Some of them would move forward. Some wouldn't. That was fine. The target was 50 percent. Half of them would see the fit and commit. The other half would go back to trying other approaches, maybe circling back someday when they were ready.

Either way, Alan would have given them value. He would have helped first. And if they did become clients, he would walk beside them as they transformed their businesses and their lives, just as his mentors had walked beside him.

His phone buzzed. A text from a name he didn't immediately recognize, then remembered: Danielle, from the Boot Camp class two months ago. She'd reached out after QCE, asking if she could pick his brain sometime.

Hey, Alan. Sorry to bother you. Having a rough week. Lost my first real prospect after the 90-Minute. They said they loved it but "weren't ready." Starting to wonder if I'm cut out for this. Any wisdom?

Alan smiled and picked up the phone to call her. He could have texted back, but he remembered what those early months felt like. The doubt. The head trash. The loneliness of building something from nothing. A voice on the other end of the line mattered.

Danielle answered on the first ring, surprised he'd called.

"You're not bothering me," Alan said before she could apologize. "This is my favorite part of the work. Truly."

He listened as she poured out her frustration. When she finished, he shared something Sue had told him years ago, back when he was the one wondering if he'd made a terrible mistake.

"The scarcity you're feeling right now? It's not real. It's just fear wearing a clever disguise. There are more companies that need this than all of us could ever serve. Your only job is to keep showing up."

The call lasted fifteen minutes. By the end, Danielle sounded lighter. She thanked him three times before hanging up.

Alan set the phone down, still smiling. A few years ago, he'd been exactly where Danielle was. Scared. Uncertain. Wondering if anyone would ever hire him. Now he got to be the voice on the other end of the line, passing along what had been passed to him.

The cycle continued. That was the whole point.

* * *

Sarah appeared in the doorway.

"Good call?" she asked.

"A referral from Eileen Sharp. Construction company. Classic case of hitting the ceiling."

"Another one for the list?"

Alan nodded. "Another one for the list."

She crossed the room and sat on the edge of his desk, looking at the photos arranged on the bookshelf behind him. Their wedding photo. The kids at various ages. A picture from last year's family vacation, the first real vacation they'd taken since he'd started his practice.

Alan's gaze drifted to the shelf below the photos, where an orange three-ring binder sat among his business books. The spine was creased now, the color faded from years of afternoon sun through the office window. His Boot Camp manual. He'd kept it within arm's reach since the day he'd come home from Detroit, a reminder of where the journey had started. Sometimes, before a difficult session, he still pulled it down and flipped through the pages, touching the notes he'd scribbled in the margins, remembering what it felt like to be a beginner.

"You seem happy," she said.

"I am happy."

"That's still strange to me sometimes. After all those years of watching you carry RTS on your shoulders, seeing you like this… " She shook her head. "It's like you became a different person."

"I didn't become a different person. I became the person I was supposed to be. I just didn't know how to get there until I found EOS."

Sarah reached over and straightened the frame holding his milestone anniversary plaque from EOS Worldwide. "Do you ever miss it? Running your own company?"

Alan considered the question. He'd built RTS from nothing. He'd employed dozens of people. He'd created something real and valuable and lasting. Walking away from that had been the hardest decision of his life.

"I miss parts of it," he admitted. "The camaraderie. The sense of building something. The relationships with my team."

"But?"

"But I was never supposed to run that company forever. I was supposed to learn from it. To be shaped by it. And then to take everything I learned and use it to help other people avoid the mistakes I made." He paused. "That's what I do now. Every time I sit down with a leadership team, I'm giving them twenty years of hard-won wisdom. I'm helping them skip the trial and error and go straight to what works."

"And that's enough?"

Alan looked at her. "It's more than enough. It's everything."

* * *

That evening, after dinner, Alan retreated to his office one more time. He pulled up his calendar and looked at the weeks ahead.

Three quarterly sessions. Two Vision Building days. A 90-Minute Meeting with John Fredrickson's team. His T-Group call. The monthly connector coffee that had become a cornerstone of his business development rhythm. This month, it was Mike Henderson, the Roundtable friend who had introduced him to Steve Polanski all those years ago. Mike was still sending referrals, still believing in what Alan did. Some relationships just kept compounding.

The T-Group call was with the same four people he'd started with. Robert Kim was still there, running a thriving practice in Milwaukee now, still delivering the kind of quiet wisdom that had helped Alan through his darkest moments. "Trust the route," Robert still said whenever one of them was tempted to deviate. They'd been holding each other accountable for all these years. That was the power of the community.

Seventeen clients now, each one at a different stage of their EOS journey. Some were just starting out, still skeptical, still learning to trust the process. Others were years in, running their own sessions, reaching out occasionally when they hit a tough issue or needed a tune-up. A few had graduated entirely, carrying the system forward on their own, sending referrals back to Alan whenever they met a frustrated entrepreneur who needed help.

Steve Polanski had been one of those graduates. Alan's very first client, the HVAC company in Eden Prairie, where he'd learned to enter the danger. Steve had run on EOS for two years, transformed his leadership team, found the Integrator Dana had never wanted to be, and eventually graduated to running his own sessions. Now Steve was one of Alan's best connectors, sending a warm lead every few months. "You changed my business," Steve had told him at their last coffee. "Least I can do is help you change someone else's."

This was The EOS Life.

Doing what he loved. With people he loved. Making a huge difference. Being compensated appropriately. With time for other passions.

He'd chased that vision for years without knowing what it was called. He'd glimpsed it in Sue Hawkes's calm confidence, in the stories of entrepreneurs who had broken through their ceilings, in the promise of a system that actually worked.

Now he was living it. Not perfectly. Not without challenges. But authentically, sustainably, in a way that honored both his gifts and his limitations.

The path to mastery has no destination.

He was still walking. He would always be walking. And that, he had finally learned, was exactly as it should be.

Alan closed his laptop, turned off the office light, and went to join his family.

Tomorrow would bring new challenges, new clients, and new opportunities to help entrepreneurs get what they wanted from their businesses and their lives. But tonight, he was simply grateful.

Grateful for the journey that had brought him here. Grateful for the community that had supported him. Grateful for the system that had given him a way to make a difference.

And grateful, most of all, for the chance to keep walking the path.

One step at a time. One client at a time. One day at a time.

The way it was always meant to be.

A NOTE FROM THE AUTHOR

To My Fellow EOS Implementers (or Future)

IF YOU'VE MADE it this far, you've walked alongside Alan Roth as he transformed from a frustrated entrepreneur to an EOS Implementer living The EOS Life. My hope is that his story resonates with your own journey or the one you're about to begin.

But before you close this book, I want to share something important. Something that goes beyond the story.

Alan's journey is fiction. The principles that guided him are not.

Everything Alan learned, struggled with, and ultimately embraced comes from the real culture of our EOS Implementer Community. The Core Values he internalized, the plumbing that makes EOS work, and the call to stay humble, pure, and abundance-minded are as real and vital today as they were when Gino Wickman and Don Tinney first began building this community.

Let me remind you of what we stand for.

Our Core Values

Be Humbly Confident. We earn confidence by preparing obsessively for every session, every meeting, every interaction. We know our stuff. We believe in what we do. And yet we remain humble about it, grateful for the chance to help. We're just real, down-to-earth people, always respectful. We abhor arrogance. We think of ourselves less, not think less of ourselves.

Grow or Die. We are obsessed with learning, growing, and reaching. We love the discomfort of trying new things, of challenging ourselves and others. We are far more afraid of contentment with the status quo than we are of the uncertainty that comes with growth. The path to mastery has no destination. We embrace that truth and find joy in the endless journey.

Help First. We believe you must deliver value before you can ask anything in return. We are givers at our core, and Help First is baked into everything we do. That's why the content is freely available in books and on the website. That's why the 90-Minute Meeting is free. That's why we deliver a great session before asking for payment. We believe that when we give to each other and to our clients, we all win.

Do the Right Thing. This is about integrity. About doing what's right because it's right, as if your mother were watching your every move. We develop deep relationships with our clients. We know we could sometimes talk them into an extra paid session, but we don't, because that's not what's right for them. Money never leads our thinking. Doing the right thing does. No amount of money is worth betraying a trust.

Do What You Say. If we've made a promise, we always deliver. We show up on time. We fully deliver what we commit to. We take responsibility and blame no one. We finish what we start. It's okay to say no, but once we say yes, we follow through.

These aren't just words on a page. They're the foundation of everything we do. When you embody these values, your clients feel it. Your community feels it. And you feel it in the quality of your work and the fulfillment of your life.

Why EOS Works: The Plumbing

There's a story we tell at Boot Camp about Mongolian plumbing. During World War II, the Russians pulled Mongolians from their huts and marched them through Berlin. The Mongolians saw buildings with shiny fixtures that, when turned, produced water like magic. Their huts didn't have such things, so they stole the fixtures. They mounted them on the walls of their huts, but no water came out.

The moral: they could steal the fixtures, but they couldn't steal the plumbing.

EOS has fixtures that anyone can see: the V/TO, The Accountability Chart, the Scorecard, The Meeting Pulse. But what makes EOS truly work is the plumbing underneath. The philosophy, the psychology, and the approach cannot be copied by simply reading a book or downloading a template.

Here is some of that plumbing:

The way we teach. Context, facilitate, conclude. We take clients to the end result first so their minds can grasp what it will look like. We facilitate rather than lecture. We conclude with clarity and commitment.

Our session guarantee. We risk our check. If the client doesn't feel they received value, they don't pay. This weeds out most of our competition and demonstrates our confidence in what we deliver.

We enter the danger. We walk into potential conflict because we are fanatical about resolution and comfortable with conflict. We go there when we see eye rolls. We don't always know the outcome, but we trust the process.

We join forces with them. High trust. We've got their backs. We're welcomed into their organizations not as outsiders but as partners in their success.

We are not consultants. We don't position ourselves as futurists or experts on their business. We don't have all the answers. *The answer is always in the room.* We don't create dependence. We teach, coach, and facilitate. We implement a system that creates independence.

We sell. We're persuading people at every step to do something they'll be thankful for in the long run. Selling is helping.

We don't solve it for them. We have to be masterful to help them come up with their own solutions. We listen. We help them solve their own problems. Like therapy, they always have the answer.

Traction first, vision second. We do the tough stuff first. Any other way would be a disservice.

We work ourselves out of a job. Our clients graduate, and we celebrate that. We're comfortable running out of things to teach them.

We don't treat symptoms. We solve problems at the root. We work with entire leadership teams, not individuals. It always comes back to one of the Six Key Components.

It's simple. EOS will always be simple. The 20/80 rule, always. We are constantly honing and refining to get maximum results in the least amount of time.

There is a high level of accountability. Execution. Traction. Getting it done. We have an obsession with concluding. We make them do it.

We help first, always. We expect nothing until we have first created value.

Our client selection. We stay true to our target market. Entrepreneurial leadership teams that are open-minded, respectful, appreciative, growth-oriented, frustrated, want help, and are willing to be open, honest, and vulnerable.

This is our secret sauce. This is why it works. Like the Green Bay Packers dynasty of the late 1960s, everyone knows where we're going with the ball. They still can't stop us.

The Call to Stay the Course

Here is my wish for you.
Three to five years from now, I hope you remain:

Abundance-minded. No scarcity thinking. Believe that there is enough for everyone. When you meet a fellow Implementer, see a colleague, not a competitor. When you have more leads than you can handle, refer them generously. When another Implementer succeeds, celebrate with them. The pie is not fixed. The more we give, the more there is for all of us.

Pure. The world wants EOS in its purest form. If you teach EOS 100 percent pure, you will get better results for your clients, generate more referrals for yourself, and create a bigger impact on the world. Don't dilute it. Don't customize it beyond recognition. Don't add your own special twist that compromises the integrity of the system. Trust what works.

Humble. Stay humble. Three years from now, some of you will become heroes to your clients. You'll be making $500,000 or more a year. You'll start to feel like you've figured it all out. When that happens, remember what brought you here. Stay nice. Stay grounded. Stay grateful. The moment you become cocky is the moment you start to slide.

If we all collectively stay abundance-minded, pure, and humble, ten years from now, we will be unstoppable. We will put a huge dent in the universe. No one will be able to touch us.

But if we start to slide, if we become scarcity-minded, impure, and arrogant, it will be the beginning of the end.

The choice is ours. Every day. Every session. Every interaction.

The Path Forward

Alan's story ends with a phone call from John Fredrickson. But really, his story doesn't end at all. The path to mastery has no destination. He's still walking it, one client at a time, one session at a time, one day at a time.

So are you.

Whether you're a new Implementer just out of Boot Camp, a Certified veteran with hundreds of sessions under your belt, or someone considering whether this path is right for you, the invitation is the same:

Stay on the path. Trust the process. Do the work.

Follow the 4-2-1 BizDev Checklist every week, especially when things are going well. Build relationships, not transactions. Help first, always. Enter the danger when you see it. Work yourself out of a job with every client.

And when you drift, because you will drift, come back. Come back to the checklist. Come back to the community. Come back to the Core Values that define who we are and what we stand for.

The EOS Life is real. I've seen hundreds of Implementers achieve it. Alan's journey is a composite of their stories, their struggles, and their triumphs. If they can do it, you can do it.

But only if you stay humble. Stay pure. Stay abundance-minded.

The world needs what we do. Entrepreneurs are out there right now, lying awake at night, frustrated with their businesses, wondering if there's a better way. They need someone to hand them a business card and say, "Call this person. They can help."

Be that person. Be the Implementer who changes their lives.

And never forget: We're all in this together. Iron sharpens iron. Help First is not just a slogan. It's how we win.

Thank you for reading Alan's story. Now go write your own.

With gratitude and respect,

Mark O'Donnell
Visionary, EOS Worldwide

What's Next

Alan Roth's story continues in **Get a Grip** *by Gino Wickman and Mike Paton, where you'll meet John Fredrickson, Eileen Sharp, and the Swan Services leadership team as they experience their own EOS transformation, guided by the Implementer whose journey you've just witnessed.*

GLOSSARY

EOS TERMS

* * *

3-Year Picture
A vivid description of what the organization will look like three years from now, including revenue, profit, measurables, and what it will "look and feel like." Part of the Vision/Traction Organizer.

10-Year Target
A long-range, energizing goal that gives everyone in the organization a shared finish line to work toward. Should be specific and measurable.

90-Day World®
The EOS concept that human beings can only focus effectively for about 90 days at a time. This is why Rocks are set quarterly and why the EOS Process works in 90-day cycles.

90-Minute Meeting
The initial meeting between an EOS Implementer and a prospective client's leadership team. Covers four steps: About Us, About You, The Tools, and The Process. Free of charge, with no obligation.

Annual Planning
A full-day session held once per year to review the prior year, refresh the V/TO, and set Rocks and goals for the coming year.

Core Focus
The combination of an organization's Purpose/Cause/Passion (why you exist) and Niche (what you do better than anyone else). Defines what the organization should and shouldn't be doing.

Core Values
A small set of essential and timeless guiding principles that define the organization's culture. Used to hire, fire, review, reward, and recognize people. Three to seven is the rule of thumb.

EOS® (Entrepreneurial Operating System®)
A complete set of simple concepts and practical tools used by leadership teams to get what they want from their businesses.

EOS Implementer®
A trained professional who helps leadership teams implement EOS in their organizations. Implementers teach, coach, and facilitate. They don't consult.

Focus Day®
The first full-day session in the EOS Process. Covers Hitting the Ceiling, the Accountability Chart, Rocks, the Meeting Pulse, and the Scorecard.

GWC®
Gets it, Wants it, and has the Capacity to do it. The three requirements for someone to be in the Right Seat. All three must be "yes."

Help First™
One of the EOS Core Values: leading with generosity, offering assistance, insight, or support to others without expecting something in return. The idea is to prioritize helping entrepreneurs, peers, and clients succeed before focusing on personal gain or transactions.

Hitting the Ceiling™
The natural phenomenon that occurs when an organization, department, or individual stops growing. Requires mastering the Five Leadership Abilities (Simplify, Delegate, Predict, Systemize, Structure) to break through.

IDS® (Identify, Discuss, Solve)
The Issues Solving Track used to solve problems at the root. Requires identifying the real issue, discussing it openly, and solving it so it goes away forever.

Integrator
The person who harmoniously integrates the major functions of the business, runs the day-to-day operations, and holds the leadership team accountable. The glue that holds the organization together.

Issues List
A running list of all obstacles, barriers, and problems that need to be solved. Issues are prioritized and solved using IDS during Level 10 Meetings and session days.

Level 10 Meeting®
A weekly leadership team meeting that follows a specific agenda designed to keep teams focused, aligned, and solving issues. Rated 1-10 at the end; the goal is consistent 10s.

Quarterly
A full-day session held every 90 days to review Rocks, refresh the V/TO, and set new Rocks for the coming quarter. Also called a Quarterly Session or Q&A.

QCE® (Quarterly Collaborative Exchange®)
A gathering of EOS Implementers for learning, sharing best practices, and community building. Held quarterly in various locations.

Right People, Right Seats
The EOS framework for ensuring you have the right people (who share your Core Values) in the right seats (who GWC their roles). You must have both.

Rocks
The three to seven most important priorities for the next 90 days. Set at the company level and the individual level. Designed to be specific, measurable, and attainable.

Scorecard
A weekly report containing five to fifteen high-level numbers that give the leadership team an absolute pulse on the business. Helps predict and identify issues early.

Six Key Components®
The six components that must be strengthened to build a great organization: Vision, People, Data, Issues, Process, and Traction.

T-Group
A small group of three to five EOS Implementers who meet regularly to hold each other accountable, share challenges, and support each other's growth. "Iron sharpens iron."

The Accountability Chart®
A tool that clarifies the right structure for an organization, defines every seat, and identifies who is accountable for what. Unlike traditional org charts, it focuses on function and accountability rather than ego or history.

The EOS Life®
Doing what you love, with people you love, making a huge difference, being compensated appropriately, and having time for other passions.

The Meeting Pulse®
The regular rhythm of meetings that keeps an organization aligned and accountable. Includes the weekly Level 10 Meeting and quarterly and annual planning sessions.

The People Analyzer®
A tool used to evaluate whether someone is a "Right Person" (shares Core Values) in the "Right Seat" (GWC). Uses +, +/-, and - ratings for Core Values and Yes/No for GWC.

V/TO® (Vision/Traction Organizer®)
A two-page document that captures an organization's vision by answering eight questions. When complete, the entire leadership team is 100 percent on the same page.

Vision Building® Day
Two full-day sessions (VB1 and VB2) that follow the Focus Day. Used to complete the V/TO and ensure the leadership

team is fully aligned on where the organization is going and how it will get there.

Vision, Traction, Healthy™
A simple set of words for framing the three abilities we believe companies need to master if they want to build great and enduring businesses. Vision: get your leadership team 100% on the same page with where you are going and how you'll get there. Traction: Build discipline and accountability so your team executes consistently. Healthy: Strengthen your leadership team into a healthy, functional, cohesive team.

Visionary
The person who has the ideas, the relationships, and the big-picture vision for the organization. Often the founder or entrepreneur. Typically paired with an Integrator.

* * *

For more information on EOS and its tools, visit eosworldwide.com or read **Traction** *by Gino Wickman.*

Protected IP

You can only bang your head against it until something breaks.[IP]

As goes the leadership team, so goes the rest of the organization.[IP]

Running the business on facts and figures instead of feelings and egos.[IP]

Real change doesn't come from someone handing you answers.[IP]

The answer is always in the room.[IP]

The things that got you here won't get you to the next level.[IP]

Most entrepreneurial companies are complex when they should be simple.[IP]

When everything is important, nothing is important.[IP]

A thousand small steps in the same direction.[IP]

Purity is what protects the client.[IP]

We don't treat symptoms. We solve problems at the root.[IP]

ABOUT THE AUTHOR

MARK O'DONNELL IS the Visionary and CEO of EOS Worldwide, where he leads a global community of over 800 EOS Implementers who have helped more than 27,000 entrepreneurial companies get what they want from their businesses.

Mark's entrepreneurial journey began at 29, and he has since built and sold nine companies for seven figures, earning a spot on the Inc. 5000 list thirteen times and achieving Inc.'s Honor Roll. But he's quick to admit that his failures—including ventures in landscaping, furniture, coding boot camps, HVAC, and a 660-acre Wyoming ranch—taught him more than his wins. It was the chaos inside one of his "successful" companies that led Mark to EOS. With teams fighting fires daily, goals being set and ignored, and growth hitting a ceiling, he knew there had to be a better way. That search transformed not only his businesses but his life's work.

As an Expert EOS Implementer, Mark has personally worked with about 100 companies and conducted more than 500 full-day sessions, helping clients achieve an average growth rate of 34%. Under his leadership, EOS Worldwide has grown from $12 million to $40 million in revenue and earned three consecutive years on the Inc. 5000.

Mark is the co-author of People: Dare to Build an Intentional Culture and Data: Harness Your Numbers to Go From Uncertain to Unstoppable, both part of the Traction Library's EOS Mastery Series. He holds an MBA from Northeastern University's D'Amore-McKim School of Business and is an alumnus of The Wharton School at the University of Pennsylvania.

Mark lives in the Greater Philadelphia area, where he continues to help entrepreneurs build stronger businesses and freer lives.

EOS

ENTREPRENEURIAL
OPERATING SYSTEM®

GET A GRIP ON YOUR BUSINESS

WITH THE ENTREPRENEURIAL OPERATING SYSTEM®

EOSWorldWide.com